HOW TO
START A
BUSINESS
WITHOUT ANY
MONEY

HOW TO
START A
BUSINESS
WITHOUT ANY
MONEY

RACHEL BRIDGE

4 6 8 10 9 7 5

First published in the United Kingdom in 2012 by
Virgin Books, an imprint of Ebury Publishing
A Random House Group Company

Addresses for companies within The Random House Group Limited can be found at
www.randomhouse.co.uk/offices.htm

The Random House Group Limited Reg. No. 954009

A CIP catalogue record for this book is available from the British Library.

The Random House Group Limited supports The Forest Stewardship
Council® (FSC®), the leading international forest-certification organisation.
Our books carrying the FSC label are printed on FSC®-certified paper.
FSC is the only forest-certification scheme supported by the leading
environmental organisations, including Greenpeace. Our
paper procurement policy can be found at
www.randomhouse.co.uk/environment

MIX
Paper from
responsible sources
FSC® C016897

Printed and bound in Great Britain by Clays Ltd, St Ives plc

Typeset in ITC Giovanni Std by Palimpsest Book Production Limited,
Falkirk, Stirlingshire

ISBN: 9780753540879

To buy books by your favourite authors and register for offers, visit www.randomhouse.co.uk

For Jack and Harry

CONTENTS

ACKNOWLEDGEMENTS

Entrepreneurs are my very favourite people in the world and it has been an absolute joy to be able to spend so much time meeting and talking to them while writing this book. Thank you so much to everyone for their time and generosity in sharing their experiences, insights and thoughts.

A big thank you to my publisher, Ed Faulkner, and everyone at Virgin Books, and to my agent Pat Lomax, for being so supportive.

I would also really like to thank my family for their support and good advice, particularly my mother and sister who were so helpful in reading early versions of the manuscript.

Thank you also to Jo Sensini, Jo Wilmot, Aneesh Varma, Pete Bulley, Matthew Pryke, Tony Walford, Lara Morgan and Tim Roupell – your thoughts and wisdom were always very much appreciated.

Finally, once again a really big hug to Harry and Jack, for making every single day special.

Rachel Bridge
Rachelbridge.com
@rachelbridge100
London

INTRODUCTION

The inspiration for writing this book came from a workshop I held for budding entrepreneurs in early 2011. I began running occasional workshops on how to start a business because so many people got in touch after reading my last book, *How to Make a Million Before Lunch* (2010), asking for my thoughts and advice on their money-making ideas.

Anyway, I arrived at this workshop with a long list of topics to talk about, but it soon became clear that all anyone really wanted to talk about was how to get their hands on some money to start their business. The banks weren't interested in lending to people without a track record in running a venture, and it was not easy to borrow money from friends and family in such an uncertain economic climate with so many jobs and pensions under threat. There was little appetite either for the traditional funding routes of remortgaging the family home or racking up huge debts on credit cards, even assuming both were still options. With housing prices falling, credit card interest rates so high and fewer opportunities to transfer money from one credit card to another offering a zero per cent transfer deal – another regular entrepreneur standby – all the old options seemed to have become too risky and unappetising.

But as we talked about the difficulty of finding funding for a start-up business, it suddenly struck me that, actually, we were having entirely the wrong conversation. We shouldn't be talking about how and where to get funding, we should be talking about how to start a business without needing funding in the first place. Surely that would be a lot more useful?

Just think about it for a minute. If you didn't actually need to borrow money to get your business off the ground – whether from the bank, or from your family, or elsewhere – then how much simpler and less daunting the whole process would be. You wouldn't have the burden of a huge debt hanging over you from day one, you wouldn't need to make loan repayments every month – plus interest and charges – and you wouldn't need to worry about how and whether you were actually going to be able to do that. Or worry about whether the bank would suddenly decide to pull the plug on your venture.

And without the need for a loan from your family and friends you could stop worrying about what would happen if you lost all their money and wrecked their lives.

Well, of course that all sounds lovely. Who wouldn't want to do that? The big question is whether it can really be done. The answer is yes, it can, and this book will show you how.

Certainly, some businesses do need a lot of money to start up. Opening a shop, building a factory and drilling for oil, to name just three. Some businesses start off in debt because they have had to pay for everything upfront and their customers take forever to pay them, so they are always effectively running to catch up. And some businesses take forever to build up to sufficient critical mass and get to a point at which they can at last begin to make money.

But others don't.

So why not actively seek out those ventures which don't have big upfront costs, which don't need lots of money to run, and which start making money from day one because customers pay them in advance? Why not simply stack all the odds in your favour?

This approach does require a bit of radical thinking. You may need to start smaller than you had imagined, for instance. Or rethink the type of product or service you are selling, and how you sell it. But the reward will be that you actually get to start a business of your own, rather than endlessly dreaming about it. And you get to do it in a much less scary way, without the financial risk and the sleepless nights.

Which means this book is for budding entrepreneurs of all ages and stages – it is for students trying to find a way to fund their way through college and create a job for themselves at the end; it is for retired people who have discovered that their pension pot has shrunk while they were not looking; and it is for people whose jobs are at risk, or who have lost their job, or who are at home trying to juggle making money with bringing up children. And it is for anyone who has ever dreamed of starting a business but thought, no, I can't afford to do it.

Even better, I am not just going to tell you how others

did it – I am going to tell you how I did it myself. Throughout this book you will be able to follow the progress of my own start-up, Entrepreneur Things, which sells inspiring products for entrepreneurs. It cost next to nothing to get off the ground and you can check it out for yourself at Entrepreneurthings.com. It's a teeny tiny business at the moment and still very much a work in progress, but it means that as well as telling you about how other people did it, I will also tell you how I did it – how I *am* doing it – and show you step by step just how easy it is to get started. And how to avoid the pitfalls, because, of course, I experienced some of them, too. After all, it wouldn't be entrepreneurship if it wasn't a roller-coaster ride.

There is an enduring myth that you need a lot of money to start a business. That it is a route open only to those with means, or access to them. But, really, you don't. You just need to choose wisely, to make the most of new technology and new ways of communicating, and above all to remember that for every decision you make there are two paths to choose between – the one which costs money and the one which doesn't.

I recently had a meeting with someone I wanted to stay in touch with, but when he offered me his business card I didn't have one of my own to give him. So while we were getting ready to leave I simply typed his email address into my BlackBerry and sent him an instant email saying hello and including my phone number and website address. A million times better than handing over a business card which he will instantly lose because my details are now sitting in his email inbox and he will always be able to search for them. He sent a short email back a few hours later and with that we were linked forever in cyberspace. It was completely free, too.

So the message of this book is, if you really want to start a business, don't let lack of money put you off. Just do it anyway. Yes, you could wait for the good economic times to roll again any time soon, but there are no guarantees that will happen and anyway by then the opportunity may have been lost forever. Don't let external factors stop you – acknowledge them, adapt and jump right in. You don't need money to get going, you just need to adopt the right attitude and think about things in a slightly different way.

And remember: the very best thing about starting a business with no money is that if it fails – and some will – then you will have lost nothing. You will have gained experience and self-knowledge – and the only thing you will have lost is the fear that your life was passing you by, and the fear that you would never get round to following your dream.

CHAPTER 1

HOW TO THINK FREE

When you are starting a business from scratch it can feel as if everywhere you look there are a hundred things for you to spend money on. Stop right there. Just because something is there doesn't mean you need it – and if you do need it that doesn't mean you have to spend money getting it. Here's how to get everything you need for free:

1. Work from home

There is a good reason why 60 per cent of all new businesses are started from home these days – it's free, it's convenient and it requires minimal organisation. You are already paying to live in it anyway in the form of rent or mortgage, heating and lighting, so it makes sense to take advantage of that. Designate a separate part of the house as your office – a spare room or warm garage is ideal if you have one, a corner of another room if not – set up a desk and commandeer the family laptop and the telephone landline. Be organised – keep all your business papers in one place, decide when your working day will begin and end, and make sure the rest of the household knows not to interrupt you when you are working or on the phone.

If you don't like the idea of physically working at home all day, then work away from home while using it as a base. Depending on the kind of venture you are starting up, that might mean the local café or library – make sure it provides free wifi and ideally has an electric socket so you can plug your laptop in – or it might mean other people's houses or offices. If you are providing consultancy work or IT support, for example, it makes a lot of sense for the client to provide you with a desk in their office while you work on the project. This arrangement can even work for ventures which have traditionally needed premises of their own – I have my hair cut by a hairdresser who comes to my house, for example. Handy for me, because it saves time and means I can get my hair cut in the evening when salons are closed. And handy for the hairdresser because she does not need to pay for the cost of running a bricks and mortar salon.

Celina Ong and Deborah Fiddy started their business, Gingerlily, selling high-quality silk bedding, from their respective homes in south-west London in 2003. The arrange-ment not only saved on costs, it also meant the two of them could juggle running the venture with caring for their children.

Celina, who set up her home office in the corner of her kitchen, says: 'It was a really good way to start because it meant we could begin without any overheads and could work around the needs of the children. There were just so many advantages to it.'

As the business began to grow, they were confident enough about its prospects to be able to move into proper offices. Gingerlily now has a turnover of £800,000 and their silk duvets and pillows are stocked in Harrods and Selfridges and sold via mail order and the internet all over the world.

Take a look at Enterprise Nation (enterprisenation.com) a free online network and resource for people running businesses from home where you will find advice, tips and, above all, a community to support you.

2. Use the skills you already have

What can you do that someone else might be prepared to pay for? Can you make cakes, programme a computer, paint and decorate, speak French, translate things into Mandarin? Can you teach someone how to play a musical instrument? All of these are services that other people will be prepared to pay good money for. If you possess a skill or knowledge that other people don't, or would need to invest time and money in learning for themselves, that immediately puts you at an enormous advantage.

Even better, if it is a skill you could teach others, then you have the makings of a business which could potentially grow and grow. Simon Dolan realised he was good with numbers so, after a couple of jobs working as a salesman and a short spell working for an accountancy firm, he put a £10 advert in the local paper offering to do year-end accounts for small firms for £99 and book-keeping for £10 a month. He says: 'The one thing I really knew how to do, other than selling, was accounts.'

He quickly discovered there was a demand for his services, particularly from one-person businesses such as building contractors and consultants, and gradually took on other people to help him. From that tiny start he has built an accountancy firm, SJD Accountancy, which employs fifty qualified accountants and has 10,000 clients – and has led to Simon amassing a personal fortune of £100 million.

3. Use the resources you have at your fingertips

Look around you. The chances are you already have access to all kinds of resources that you could use to start a business without even realising it. Have a car? Then you could offer a local delivery service. Have a lawnmower and garden tools? Then you could offer to mow people's lawns and start a gardening business. Have a kitchen? Then you can start making cakes or catering for parties.

When Guy Nixon started his venture, Go Native, providing short-term serviced apartments in London for overseas visitors, he had just one problem. He hardly had any serviced apartments to offer his potential clients. The plan was that people with empty properties would let them out through his business in return for an income. But in the early stages of starting out he only had the odd property owned by friends to offer. Then Guy realised he had one amazing free resource available to him – his own flat in London's fashionable Notting Hill. So he included the particulars of his flat on his website as being available to rent – and whenever a customer booked it, he and his wife and baby would go and stay with his mother. The constant upheaval was, he admits, a bit of a struggle, but the sacrifice paid off for his business. Go Native, which is based in west London, now has a turnover of £28 million.

4. Do all the work yourself – and don't pay yourself a wage

If you are starting a venture without any money, you will have to do most of the work yourself – and you will have to plough everything you earn straight back into the business. It may sound fairly thankless and pretty austere, and indeed, it will be for the first few years. But that is the only way you will be able to build up enough cash reserves to be able to invest in new equipment, or new premises, and so move the venture on from a hand-to-mouth existence to one which can really invest in its own future.

Which means it is also important to:

5. Hold on to the day job

Start your business in your spare time and only give up the day job once it has become established enough to be able to pay you a wage. Ten years ago this would have been impossible. Now, thanks to new technology and ways of communicating, it is not only possible, it is the perfect low-risk solution to starting up without any money. If the business doesn't work out, you still have your job. If it does, then the transition to being your own boss will be a lot less stressful – and a lot less risky – because the venture will already be successfully up and running.

If you do not have a day job to hold on to, then if possible get a part-time job – an evening job in a pub or supermarket, say – which will provide you with some money to contribute towards the rent or mortgage and the household bills while you are starting your business, but will still give you enough free time during the day to make phone calls and get your venture off the ground. This approach is a sensible one even if you are made redundant and are given a redundancy cheque, especially if you can find a job where you can learn more about running a business at the same time.

The government has also introduced a new enterprise allowance (NEA) scheme (details at dwp.gov.uk) for unemployed people who have been out of work for at least six months which provides a weekly allowance for twenty-six weeks plus the chance to access a loan to help with start-up costs.

When Sam Bompas and Harry Parr started making traditional English jellies for parties and events, they had no idea whether there would be enough demand from caterers to enable them to turn their venture into a profitable business. So they launched it with less than £50 each, which they spent on equipment. They initially ran the operation in their spare time from their kitchen table while Sam kept his full-time day job working for a public relations and marketing firm and Harry studied architecture full-time in his final year at college. They invested all the money they made from each order in more equipment and started creating jellies in the shape of famous buildings such as St Paul's Cathedral and the Taj Mahal. When it proved difficult to find the moulds they needed to make their jellies, they started making and selling those, too.

In the event, their jellies proved so popular that eight months after starting up the business, Sam was able to give up his day job and work on their venture full-time, as did Harry when he finished his degree. The pair now employ two people in their studio in Borough, south-east London and have a turnover of £1 million a year.

Sam says: 'The business picked up really quickly. It has just been incredible. Jellies look so spectacular and relate to childhood so they are something that people get excited about. And because we have made and eaten hundreds of thousands of jellies in the past few years, we really know how to make jellies well.'

6. Source free equipment

Get the equipment you need to start your business by seeking out second-hand stuff which someone else no longer wants. If you are lucky you might even manage to kit out your entire venture for free. If you need a free desk, chair or filing cabinet, for example, then check out Freecycle (freecycle.org), a community website set up to enable people to recycle unwanted items. You must become a member of your local Freecycle group to be able to take part in the scheme, and you must offer an item yourself first before you can ask for something being given away.

It is also worth checking out Gumtree (gumtree.com) and Craigslist (craigslist.co.uk), both of which have sections where people can offer free products and services. A quick glance at the 'freebie' section on Gumtree, for example, reveals that one person is offering free café equipment, including a coffee machine, fridge and stainless-steel counter in Marylebone, while someone else is offering free fitness equipment in Bournemouth.

7. Tap into free inspiration

If you are looking for inspiration and information for your business idea, Startup Britain (startupbritain.org), an organisation supported by the government, runs a free downloadable enterprise calendar on its website, listing all the events for entrepreneurs which are taking place month by month around the country, many of them free and open to anyone. The British Chambers of Commerce (britishchambers.org.uk) also runs free events for start-ups – contact your local chamber of commerce via their website for details of what's on and where. Smarta (smarta.com) is a free online advice and networking resource for anyone starting up a business and has lots of tips, articles and videos on its website. TED (ted.com) is a non-profit organisation which runs conferences each year focusing on technology, education and design. It has a wealth of amazing free talks and speeches from participants on its website which will inspire and inform. I particularly recommend Steve Jobs' speech 'How to live before you die'.

8. Access free research

The government has closed down the regional offices of its advisory service, Business Link, but it does still have a useful website at businesslink.gov.uk, providing free advice on every aspect of starting up a venture. The Business and IP centre at the British Library (bl.uk/bipc) is also an amazing free resource. You can access their databases, research reports for free and also book a free one hour session with one of their advisers. The Business and IP centre also runs lots of free workshops and events for start-ups. City Business Library (cityoflondon.gov.uk) is another useful place to visit, offering free information and free workshops for entrepreneurs and start-ups.

And don't forget your local library either. It will have lots of back copies of trade magazines for the industry you wish to enter, which will provide you with invaluable free insight.

9. Get a grant

Sadly there are far fewer grants around to help people start businesses than there used to be – but there are still some available so it is worth spending an evening checking them out on the internet. Many have strict criteria which you need to meet in order to be eligible to apply so check the small print first before you spend hours on an application.

The best place to start looking is the Business Support Finder, a free database on the Business Link website which lists all publicly funded sources of assistance. You can filter the results by type, sector and region.

Sue Acton managed to get a grant of £15,000 in 2009 to fund the start-up of her venture, Bubbles and Balm, which makes Fairtrade body care products such as soap bars and liquid hand wash. She discovered the existence of the grant quite by chance she says, after 'endless Googling' and was delighted to find she met the criteria. The grant was provided by Innovation Networks, a government-backed grant scheme which is funded by the European Regional Development Fund and Advantage West Midlands. It is solely for businesses with an innovative new product, process or service projects which will provide benefits to the West Midlands economy.

Sue, who runs her business from her home in Leamington Spa, used the grant to pay for ingredients, packaging and labelling for her products, which were some of the first Fairtrade body care products sold in the UK and are bottled in distinctive recyclable aluminium bottles. Her products are now sold in Waitrose supermarkets, Oxfam charity shops and high street retailers, and the enterprise has a turnover of £100,000.

She says: 'It was so fantastic to be given a grant. It meant I was able to invest in better equipment and to be much more professional in the way I set up the business. I burst into tears when I saw my products on the shelves in Waitrose. It was an amazing moment.'

If you are under thirty, check out Shell Livewire (shell-livewire.org), a social investment programme backed by Shell which offers free online advice, support and networking opportunities for sixteen- to thirty-year-olds and every month gives up to four Grand Ideas Awards of £1,000 to people starting up a business. It also gives an annual £10,000 Young Entrepreneur of the Year prize to one monthly winner. The Princes Trust (princes-trust.org.uk) also provides grants and loans to people under thirty who are long-term unemployed.

10. Learn the business skills you need for free

Want to know how to change a plug or lay laminated flooring? Want to know how to do double-entry book-keeping – or make macaroons? There is a free video on YouTube to show you how. In fact, there are hundreds of free videos on YouTube showing you how to practise all sorts of useful practical skills. Check out other free courses in your area, too – type in the word 'free' into Floodlight (floodlight.co.uk) and dozens of useful free options come up. Your local council may also offer free business sessions. Somerset County Council runs a free Business Start-up exhibition for budding entrepreneurs as part of its Business Start-up programme, for example, while Wandsworth Council offers free public procurement courses for small firms.

11. Make the most of free technology

Once you have acquired a website address for your business, set up an email account for it with your company name as the bit at the end. It will instantly make your business look professional and well established. If your venture is called Green Gardens, for example, then having the email address enquiries@greengardens.com will look a lot more professional than simply having it as greengardens@yahoo.com. You can also set it up so that an email using any word followed by @greengardens.com, such as sales@greengardens.com, marketing@greengardens.com, invoices@greengardens.com and so on, will reach you, making your tiny one-person enterprise look as big and grand as you want.

Build a free website at sites such as moonfruit.com, basekit.com or wix.com, who will also host it for free on their server. You can then forward the website address you have acquired to the site you have created. If you want to start writing a blog you can do it for free at wordpress.com or blogger.com.

Get social networking. It's free, it's easy, it's everywhere, and it is an amazing way of promoting your business without spending any money. Sign up to Twitter (twitter.com), create a Facebook page (facebook.com), and join Linkedin (linkedin.com).

12. Make use of existing local infrastructure

I recently met someone who wanted to start a chain of child-friendly cafés where under-fives could take part in creative activities while their parents looked on and drank coffee. The only problem, she said, was that it would cost a fortune to rent the cafés and kit them out and get the business off the ground. I suggested she simply turn the idea on its head instead.

There must be hundreds of cafés already up and running which are struggling in these difficult times. They might be in the wrong place, or have too much local competition, especially from the chains of Starbucks and Caffè Nero which need to work less hard at establishing a local reputation. So why not develop a capsule idea consisting of a range of children's activities, a structure and a name, and approach the owner of an ailing café and see if they would like to take your concept? The chances are they will have no money to spend on something upfront either, so why not agree an arrangement whereby you take space in the café for free, and then give the café owner a percentage of the money you charge for running your activities?

The café will also benefit from the additional sales of coffee, cakes and lunches to the parents and children. You could both try it out on a three-month basis and adapt it to meet local demand – more classes for babies perhaps, or experiment with different length classes at different times.

See? Instantly the idea is transformed from something which would cost a fortune to something which costs next to nothing – and in the process utilises unused resources and possibly regenerates and breathes life into another business, the ailing café.

ACTION PLAN

▶▶ **Find out what free local business networking groups are in your area. Join them.**

▶▶ **Think about the existing infrastructure in your area which you can take advantage of – a half-empty hotel? A little-used town hall? A theatre which is only used in the evenings?**

▶▶ **Write down a list of the resources you already have to hand, and skills you have which you could charge for.**

CHAPTER 2

IDEAS THAT WILL MAKE MONEY FAST

When I was at the Edinburgh Fringe Festival performing my one-woman show about entrepreneurs, a tiny shop opened near the theatre. It was situated in a small row of three shops well away from the main shopping streets – and it sold nothing but cushions. Every day I walked past I could see a lady sitting behind the counter waiting hopefully for a customer to come in and buy one. But no one ever did. Indeed, the whole time I was there I never saw anyone go into the shop. The cushions were handmade and they looked lovely, but there were so many reasons why the venture was all wrong. The shop was too small, it was in the wrong place, it was too daunting for customers to go into and be the only ones in there – and it only sold cushions.

And therein lay the bigger problem. Cushions are not an

impulse buy. Even if you like the look of a cushion in the window, you are unlikely to want to buy it right there and then because you would have to carry it around with you all day. I really hope that the shop is busy proving me wrong and doing really well. But it is certainly not the easiest route to success.

When starting a business without any money, you not only need to avoid upfront costs; you also need to choose a venture which will start generating cash from day one. And that means finding a product or service and a market which makes it easy for the customer to say yes, not no.

So how do you go about it? Here's how:

Choose a product or service which people need rather than want

With a big fat zero in your marketing budget, you simply don't have the time or money to wait for people to get round to buying your product or service one day in the future. You need to find something you will be able to sell from day one, which means it must be a product people really need, which doesn't cost too much and which they cannot put off buying.

You need them to need it RIGHT NOW.

About a year ago a new restaurant opened near where I live. It looked amazing and every evening it looked enticing inside, with dimmed lights and candles at each table. And every time I went past I imagined how nice it would be to spend an evening there, and I would linger over the menu outside and decide I would definitely go and eat there soon. But somehow I never quite got round to it. It stayed on my 'I'd quite like to do that one day' list, and never quite made it to the 'I absolutely have to do that now' list. And the other day I went past and realised they'd taken all the chairs and tables away and it had closed down.

My loss, but that doesn't help the owners now.

This is why you need to be very careful about the kind of research you do, and how you interpret it. Travel surveys always show that the number one dream holiday destination for British holidaymakers is Australia. No question about it: that is where we would all go, given the choice. I am dreaming about it even as I write. The beaches, the Outback, the sun, the kangaroos. The sheer fabulousness of it all. But before you all rush out and start businesses selling holidays to Australia, let's look at the other statistics, the ones which show where we REALLY go on holiday. According to the latest UK government statistics, the top five places where British people actually go on holiday overseas are:

▶▶ Spain

▶▶ France

▶▶ Irish Republic

▶▶ USA

▶▶ Italy

Not Australia. In fact, Australia doesn't even make it into the top ten. That paints a rather different picture, doesn't it?

Yes, Australia is our number one dream destination, but do we actually follow through and go there? No, because it costs a fortune, because it takes a day and night to get there and three days to recover from the jetlag, because we would need to take at least three weeks off work to make it worth our while. And because we know we would never be allowed to take three weeks off work in one go, and that even if we were it would mean we only had one week's holiday left for the rest of the year. And because even if we have the money and the time, it really is an enormous amount of money to spend just on a holiday.

It is not for nothing that a recent campaign by the Australian Tourism Commission simply showed empty idyllic beaches, with the words 'Where the bloody hell are you?' Well, we were working out just how much it was going to cost and whether we should instead be spending the money on boring but essential things such as replacing the boiler, or fixing the car, or repainting the house, that's where.

The bottom line is you can't afford to sell a product or service that people can delay and put off buying indefinitely. You will go bust. Other better funded businesses might be able to afford to wait. You can't.

Choose a product or service people instantly understand

Neither do you have the time or money to start educating potential customers about why they need your product or what it can do for them. Some people create amazing businesses by filling gaps people never knew they had in their lives. After all, who thought they needed an iPod or an iPad until they saw them and fell in love with them and realised they really did? Steve Jobs knew long before we did ourselves that we were going to love his products and would be helpless to resist when we saw them in their sleek designs and lovely shiny colours. So he spent many years and many millions inventing them, confident in his belief that one day he would be able to sell lots of them and make a great deal of money.

But you don't have time or money on your side. What might work for well-funded start-ups will not work for you. So you need to choose a product or service which people instantly 'get', otherwise it is going to be an uphill – and expensive – battle.

This is why, as a first-time entrepreneur with limited funds, you should always avoid being the first into a market. This was the problem faced by Catherine and Richard Furze. In 2009 they decided to start making and selling savoury gourmet popcorn for adults, in the belief they would be able to create a new market for a new kind of snack. Catherine came up with the idea for the product after reading about a character in a novel by the American author Lionel Shriver eating savoury popcorn, and was confident that people in the UK would also grow to love savoury, rather than sweet, flavours.

So, using personal savings of £4,000, the pair bought a popcorn-making machine from the US and got to work making popcorn, in the kitchen of their home in Consett,

County Durham. Catherine and Richard used natural ingredients to flavour the popcorn – the first four varieties they produced were fennel and chilli, Italian herb, honey and mustard, and the peculiar sounding kettle corn, which is flavoured with a mixture of sugar and salt. Then they packaged the popcorn themselves, called it Corn Again, and set about persuading local delicatessens to stock it.

It was – and still is – an enticing idea, but the problem they have constantly encountered is that people are simply not used to eating savoury popcorn. Worse, adults don't really eat popcorn anyway – not in the UK at least, where it is primarily seen as a snack for children. So adults have to be taught to enjoy their savoury popcorn, usually by tasting it themselves. And once they have got over that hurdle, they have to be taught when in their lives they might want to eat it and therefore why they might want to buy it.

Catherine and Richard have therefore had to spend an enormous amount of time and effort taking stands at food fairs around the country, so they can talk directly to prospective customers and explain their product and put out bowls of their popcorn so people can try it for themselves. Even then it has been a battle persuading people to give it a go. As Catherine says: 'We found that people were saying, oh no, savoury popcorn, that is just wrong. We couldn't get over that hump.'

Indeed, to begin with it was so hard to persuade people to try their savoury popcorn that the couple started making a sweet cinnamon spice variety, too, simply to entice people into their brand.

Catherine says: 'We discovered if we had a sweet variety

as well they would try the sweet one and then a savoury one too. It was our entry point.'

They have chalked up some successes – dozens of delicatessens around the UK now stock their popcorn, and so does the supermarket chain Asda, which sells Corn Again in nineteen stores. The additional problem now, though, is that just as customers are finally waking up to the idea of eating savoury popcorn, so too are other snack makers. Noticing the growing interest in savoury popcorn, a number of competitors have now entered the market, including the large crisp firm Tyrrells, sandwich chain, Pret a manger and newcomers Joe & Seph's and ProperCorn.

This is good news on one level, as Catherine and Richard's Corn Again brand will benefit from the growing acceptance of savoury popcorn among customers as a genuine alternative to sweet popcorn, and to other savoury snacks such as pretzels. But it is also a potentially scary scenario, too. Having worked really hard for three years trying to create a demand for savoury popcorn, Catherine and Richard are now having to watch in frustration as their idea is seized upon by others, some of whom have many times their marketing budget and distribution power, so can get their savoury popcorn into outlets with much greater speed and ease. The couple were right – they have indeed proved there is a demand for savoury popcorn, and in the process created a niche market for it – but the sad thing for them is they may not ultimately be the ones who benefit. With so many powerful competitors in the market it might not end up being Corn Again savoury popcorn that customers buy.

One day it may be that a large snack maker wishing to

enter the market will want to buy Catherine and Richard's business to give them an instant presence in the market, saving them the effort of creating a product of their own from scratch. But, being the first into a market is a scary place for start-ups on a tight budget.

Choose a well-trodden route to market

As well as choosing a product people already understand, if you are starting out with no money then you also need to choose a route to market which your customers already feel comfortable using.

When Andy Moffat decided to give up his job in finance and start brewing real ale, he had an extremely good idea of who was likely to want to buy his beer – and how – even before he had made his first barrel.

He says: 'I knew from the kind of pubs I visit that there are a number in north London which stock a good range of beers from different microbreweries throughout Britain, so they were going to be pretty happy about having a locally brewed beer. I felt there was a big opportunity.'

So he established a microbrewery in an industrial unit in north London, then he drove round to some local pubs with casks of his ale and asked the landlords if they'd like to buy some. A tried and tested route which was simple but effective because that's how beer is sold; everyone involved knew how the system worked and what was expected of them. As a result his fledgling business, The Redemption Brewing Company, now makes thirty barrels of ale a week and supplies 150 pubs around London.

Have multiple routes to market

It is always a good idea to combine two or even three routes to market in case one fails. Selling via retailers and via your own website, for example. Or via a market stall and also by mail order. That way you find out which works best and you get to reach different groups of people. And you have a fall-back option so if one route to market fails to work, you can still reach your customers, and they can still buy things from you.

Charles Hunt learnt this lesson the hard way. He started a mail order business at the age of twenty-six with £500 selling bed linen and towels. He and a friend, Claire Dyball, ran the venture from a flat in Battersea, south London. It took off and did well for eight years, achieving annual sales of £6 million. But the business was dealt a fatal blow in 2005 when a postal strike prevented catalogues reaching customers in the valuable Christmas sales period.

'They sat at Royal Mail from the end of November to the end of December and so we lost our entire Christmas trade. We lost hundreds of thousands of pounds of revenue,' says Charles.

The firm struggled on for a while but never recovered and went into administration at the beginning of 2007. Even worse, Charles had personally guaranteed the borrowings and so was left owing the bank more than £500,000.

Fortunately, Charles has since bounced back with a new online venture, Duvet and Pillow Warehouse, which has a turnover of £5 million. But the experience taught him an important lesson: 'We had too much in one basket. We had everything banked on catalogues and Royal Mail distributing them, so it took only one incident like that to knock down the business.'

Avoid high-ticket products or services

If you are starting out without much money, choose something which is relatively low-cost per unit – first because buying stock will cost you less, and second because in a tough economic climate people are reluctant to shell out for high-ticket items, at least not without carefully thinking about it first. Umbrellas are a better choice than hot tubs.

Ideally, you want a product or service that people will be prepared to buy without having to think too much about whether they can really afford it or not, and that they don't have to consult anyone else about. You should also be looking for a product which is fairly lightweight and portable – another reason why umbrellas win over hot tubs. If you are selling your products online, heavy ones will incur high delivery costs and put people off; if you are selling them in a shop, people will be deterred from buying heavy, bulky products because they can't carry them home, fit them in the car or take them on the bus (and retailers will be put off stocking them because they take up too much shelf space).

Swap fixed costs for variable ones

Fixed-cost overheads are the ones you have to pay regardless of whether or not you are actually selling anything. They are the big upfront costs of renting offices, paying business rates, paying staff, storing stock. They are relentless and unbending and have to be paid whether you are selling five units or 100 units or even no units at all.

Fixed-cost overheads are bad news for start-ups hoping to do without money. So replace fixed costs with variable costs and adopt a new model – pay as you go. Pay as you go means that all your costs – whether buying in stock or hiring staff – are linked to your sales. Which means they only have to be paid when your product or service is actually sold – and so can generate the money you need to pay them. A great example of how to do this is mywarehouse.me, a service which will take delivery of your stock, deal with your orders, pick and pack the stock and send it out to customers, without you ever having to get involved. There are no set-up fees, no fixed fees, no minimum volumes and no minimum contract. You simply pay for the service as you need it.

The good news is you are in a great position, because in order to get this right you really need to put the right structure in place at the start before you have got going. It can be difficult to unpick and redo – and shrink – the underlying cost structure once the business is up and running. The cost structure is like the architect's plan of a building – simple to tweak when the plans are just a drawing on a piece of paper and the building doesn't yet exist, a nightmare to change when the building is half built.

Ask for payment upfront

Always get your customers to pay you upfront, whether they are individuals or other companies. If that is not possible, ask for half upfront, half later. That way you know your costs are covered for the work you are doing. If you get really lucky, you can use this approach to fund your entire venture. Tony Goodwin was working for an accountancy recruitment firm when, at the age of thirty, he decided to leave to start a recruitment firm of his own. It was not great timing, however. It was the middle of a recession so no one was hiring accountants.

Then he noticed that multinationals such as Coca-Cola and Mars were starting operations in Eastern Europe and Russia in the wake of the collapse of communism. 'I thought they must need accountants and staff' he says.

He began calling them and managed to persuade four companies to pay him upfront retainers of £2,000 each to find accountants for them. That gave him £8,000 which he used to start his business. He called his venture Antal – his name in Hungarian – and got to work, running the enterprise from a small office in Putney, south-west London.

His friends thought he was mad. 'A good friend of mine said, Tony, you can't speak Hungarian or Polish or Russian, what on earth are you doing trying to recruit into these countries? I said I think English will be the main language, and, fortunately for me, it was.'

Initially he found the accountants to fill the vacant positions by looking among the expat community in the UK for people who were keen to return home. He then switched to recruiting locally and by 1994 he was opening offices overseas.

By 2007 the Russian operation was doing so well that Goodwin was able to sell it for close to £18 million, of which 80 per cent went to him. Today the company operates in 33 countries and has 100 offices, of which 79 are franchised. It now has an annual turnover of £40 million and employs 500 people.

However, there are some business structures you should avoid at all costs when starting up with no money:

Avoid ventures which need to reach a critical mass before they can get going

Do not start a venture which requires a certain number of people to sign up to it before it can start to function properly – and start making money. This rules out ideas such as a dating site or a holiday home rental site. No one is going to want to join a site which only offers the choice of three people to meet. Although businesses such as these can be successful, you do need money to support the business from its launch to the point at which it starts generating cash of its own; without any money, you will seriously struggle.

Avoid online businesses which rely on advertising to make money

It is an appealing idea to create a website whose sole purpose is to offer information – a database of useful services in your area, for example – and then make money from advertising on the site. Unfortunately the model doesn't work for small start-ups. Advertisers are not going to spend money advertising on sites few people visit, and, for the first few years at least, not enough people will be visiting yours. As a journalist I once followed the fortunes of two people who started an online sports directory providing free information about local sports clubs and courses. A lovely idea, but even two years after it was launched advertising on the site never brought in more than a few pounds a month. The venture folded soon after.

Avoid online businesses which aim to make money purely from linking to other sites

We have all accidently stumbled across these kinds of sites while looking for something else. They are filled with links to other sites and they usually look really awful. They work on the principle of affiliate marketing – generating income by providing traffic to other sites – and a lot has been written about how easy it is to throw a website like this together and then sit back while the money flows in. But if it seems too good to be true, it generally is. Internet users are increasingly wise to sites like these and so avoid them. And now Google has changed the way it ranks sites – it increasingly values content over links from other sites – to avoid them too. Don't waste your time.

How to find a good idea

So how do you come up with a winning business idea? I have covered this in more detail in previous books but basically the very best place to start is your own life. Look at the products and services you use. Is there something that really annoys you? Do you find it impossible to find the product you need in the right colour, or the right size, or at a price you are happy to pay? Is there a shop you like which is located too far away – or which is always closed when you need it? Is there a service you would be happy to pay for – gardening, computer repairs, dog walking, clothes making, book-keeping – but just can't find in your area? Is the business which provides you with a particular service hopelessly incompetent at doing the job properly and always gets it wrong? Or are they just plain rude every time you speak to them on the phone? Then there is your answer. Success in business is not about being complicated and clever, it's about finding a gap in the market for a product or service that people need – and then doing it better, faster, simpler or more efficiently.

ACTION PLAN

▶▶ Ask yourself, is your proposed product or service just something people want – or is it something they actually need? And if they need it, how long are they able to put off actually buying it? Just as importantly, do they understand why they need it? If they need it but don't realise it – dental insurance, for example, or carbon monoxide detectors – then you might still struggle to achieve sales.

▶▶ Find out more about the industry you are planning to enter – how do customers, whether individuals or businesses, generally pay for the type of products or services you will be offering? Upfront? In arrears? Or a mixture of both?

▶▶ Consider how you are going to sell your product or service – online, offline, or a bit of both?

CHAPTER 3

PUTTING IT INTO PRACTICE

I've been longing to start a business of my own without any money so I can see for myself what works and what doesn't, and what pitfalls to avoid. The idea of creating something special from scratch is incredibly exciting and now I have the opportunity to do it.

After giving it some thought, I decide I want to sell a product rather than a service, because I want something I can both sell online and in person at the events and workshops I speak at. I also want to find something which in some way reflects the work I do and the people I meet so that I have a real connection with what I am selling.

To help me decide what this amazing product will be, I make a list of things it should and shouldn't be. You should do this, too. Some are common sense, some are things which suit my circumstances and temperament:

▶▶ Must be non-food (lots of health and safety requirements; no desire to accidently poison anyone)

▶▶ Must be robust enough to post – but small enough to be deliverable by the postman

▶▶ Must have long shelf life

▶▶ Must not be too heavy (if you are selling them online, heavy products will incur big delivery costs and put people off; if you are selling them in a shop, people will be deterred from buying anything they can't transport home)

▶▶ Ideally sell for around £10–£20 (don't want to give people a reason to delay buying it)

▶▶ Must be made in the UK (want to support local firms, will also appeal to more customers)

▶▶ Must be something I would like to buy myself

▶▶ Must be absolutely no possibility of injuring or killing anyone using the product

▶▶ Must not be too fashion-orientated, e.g. clothes, as the products will go out of style quickly

▶▶ Must be something I can stamp my imprint on, either in the design or the service (there needs to

be something which makes it stand out from the
competition because otherwise there will be no
reason for someone to buy it from me rather
than elsewhere)

In the middle of the night I wake up inspired: I will
sell picnic products. I love buying things like rugs and
plastic champagne glasses, and useful bowls in bright plastic
colours. Picnic products are long-life, the right price and
extremely unlikely to kill anybody.

Full of excitement, my mind starts to race. I could take
stands at county shows around the country and pack a van
full of lovely products to sell there. I could get my friends
to run the stands. I could put articles about picnics on my
website and include a top ten guide to good picnic places.
And a weather forecast. I could include links on the website
to picnic-related events such as Glyndebourne, Ascot,
Wimbledon. I could even include recipes for picnic food.

I start to think about possible names. Picnic Things?
Picnic Stuff? Something more esoteric? The name has to
work both as a stand-alone name and as a dot com name.
Which, sadly, wereallgoingonasummerholiday.com doesn't.
I decide I want a name which does exactly what it says. I
go to Lowcostnames (lowcostnames.co.uk), which sells
domain names, and check out what is available. I see that
I could buy thingstotakeonapicnic.co.uk (£6.50 plus VAT
for two years) and thingstotakeonapicnic.com (£20 for two
years), for example.

I'm already thinking about how I could expand my
as yet non-existent business, so I could also buy

thingstotaketothebeach.co.uk and thingstotaketothebeach.com (another £26.50). Thinking even bigger, I could also buy thingstotake.com and thingstotakeplaces.co.uk and things-totakeplaces.com, as possible umbrella names for the empire which is expanding by the second in my mind.

However, thingstotake.co.uk has already gone, and there is really no point in getting just the dot com ending without the dot co.uk ending, and vice versa, no matter how nice the name is. All is not lost, though, as the thingstotake.co.uk website has not yet been developed, so in a spirit of exploration I go to Sedo (sedo.co.uk), a site where you can buy and sell domain names which have already been taken, and offer the current owner £50 to buy it from him. He responds with a counter offer of €250,000 (around £200,000). Hmm. I pass.

One word of warning – it is incredibly easy to buy up far too many website domain names when you are on a site like Lowcostnames, so if you are anything like me you may need to exercise some restraint. I'm not sure why they appeal so much – the fear that someone else will buy it first combined with the excitement of what the website could turn into, maybe, together with the fact that they only cost a few pounds each and that it's just so easy to click and buy them. I'm not even going to admit how many website domain names I personally own, all bought in a fit of excitement about their future potential. Chris Orrell, the founder of Hotelstayuk.com, a hotel-room finding website, confesses to owning more than 250 domain names. Then again he has managed to turn some of them into successful businesses which together have a turnover of £3.4 million.

Anyway, back to my picnic venture. I start writing a list of the picnic products I could sell. Big wake-up call number one. I'd been thinking about plastic champagne glasses and rugs and maybe a couple of picnic baskets and some plates. Maybe even a pocket hand warmer. I rather like them. But it turns out there are hundreds of picnic products out there. I make a list of possible product categories and it looks like this:

▶▶ Picnic rugs and blankets

▶▶ Hampers and cool bags. Ice blocks

▶▶ Plate and cutlery sets

▶▶ Plastic wine and champagne glasses. Tumblers

▶▶ Plastic jugs and serving bowls

▶▶ Salad servers and serving spoons

▶▶ Plastic storage boxes. Cake boxes and stands

▶▶ Wine coolers. Wine carriers. Wine stoppers. Corkscrews. Wine buckets

▶▶ Parasols and sunshades. Windbreaks

▶▶ Folding chairs. Inflatable chairs. Shooting sticks. Folding tables

▶▶ Children's games. Cricket. Croquet. Boules.
Buckets and spades

▶▶ Hand warmers. Thermal blankets. Portable stoves

▶▶ Disposable barbecues

Hmm. That is a lot of products. Even supposing my little business decides to stock only some of these products, that is many different lines of stock to manage and control, and therefore potentially many different suppliers.

Still, maybe there is a wholesaler somewhere where one can buy every kind of picnic product, I think. A kind of one-stop shop. So I go online to find one. Big wake-up call number two. I only want to sell products made in the UK, both to support UK firms and also because I think it will be a great selling point. But the only British-made products I can find are individually handcrafted products such as rugs. No plastic champagne glasses here.

So I start Googling and soon I discover a wholesaler in China who sells picnic products of every kind, and they look really cheap. For a moment I am tempted to send him an email, but then I come to my senses. First, the whole point is to buy British, and second it would be easy to get burnt dealing with a supplier I know nothing about.

I decide to check out the competition. It turns out there is a lot of competition and all of it big. Asda, Argos, Tesco, John Lewis. All selling a good selection of cheap and cheerful picnic products. The only way to stand out from that crowd would be to:

▶▶ sell such a wide range of picnic products that customers would come to you because it would save traipsing around lots of different shops;

▶▶ create a really strong brand so customers wanting to buy picnic things would immediately know you were the place to go.

The other big problem with selling picnic products, of course, is that it is a seasonal enterprise. Customers are only going to want to buy your products for about five months of the year, from, say, May to September. If you are lucky. If it rains all summer you are hardly going to sell anything.

So picnic products are out. What other ideas do I have? I think about how successful entrepreneurs choose what products or services to sell. Time and time again they choose to sell something they know a lot about, or have a passion for, or have a strong connection with. Austen Pickles, founder of Buxton Pickles, which makes tailored women's clothing for high street stores such as Next, Jaeger and Hobbs, says he decided to start his business because he already knew the industry inside out, and because the opportunity presented itself.

Austen worked for a tailor which designed men's tailored clothing and had it made up in a factory in the Czech

Republic. When the firm decided to open a factory of its own in Hungary, Austen spotted an opportunity to use the spare capacity left in the Czech factory and start up his own firm making women's tailored clothing, so he wasn't in direct competition with his former employer. His business thrived and now has a turnover of £8 million.

It works even better if you can use your knowledge and skills to create a specialist niche in the market for yourself. The great thing about a niche is you can quickly build up a reputation for being really good at one particular thing. Hunter Jameson, a boutique financial recruitment consultancy based in Mayfair, was started in 2008 by Martin Leach. It specialises in placing accountants with firms in the food and drink, retail, film and leisure industries, primarily because those are the areas Martin and his team are most interested in. The firm now has six employees and makes hundreds of placements a year with FTSE 100 and Fortune 500 companies.

Martin says that working in such a narrow field has produced spectacular results. 'We genuinely believe that, in the recruitment market, specialisation can win the day,' he says. 'Premium people do not have time to apply for jobs, you have to go and find them. We have done a lot of work developing a deep network and mapping all the key finance operators. So when we are approached by clients, it is not a case of thinking, oh blimey, how are we going to find the people they need – we already know where they are.'

Martin adds: 'Specialisation enables us to provide a really comprehensive selection of people because we get to know them very well indeed. The fundamental thing is our knowledge of the sector.'

We Are Social, a social media agency based in Clerkenwell, central London, has also followed its interests and specialist skills to create a niche for itself – and in the process found itself right at the heart of the current obsession with Twitter and Facebook.

The firm, which advises businesses on how to grow by using social media, started in 2008 with two people and now has offices in Paris, Milan and Sydney and more than seventy staff.

Nathan McDonald, who founded the firm with Robin Grant, says they saw the potential for the venture after seeing social media take off in America: 'We spotted a trend and tried to position ourselves as well as possible for that trend. Businesses are turning to the internet and social media to be more effective and we are expecting the growth to continue.'

The answer for me, I realise, is to forget about picnic products and find something else I love which I can start off in a very small way and make my own.

Suddenly I know what to do. I want to sell products which will inspire and encourage budding entrepreneurs. I am passionate about entrepreneurship, and its importance both on an individual level and for society as a whole, and I'm passionate about supporting entrepreneurs to be the best they can be. It would be wonderful to create a business which somehow reflects this.

A friend comes round for Sunday lunch and brings his

new girlfriend with him. She tells me she has started designing mugs with pictures of historical figures on them. A light bulb goes on in my head. Mugs. MUGS. I will sell mugs which say ENTREPRENEUR on them in bold letters. They will be both practical and inspiring, and they will be perfect for fledgling entrepreneurs sitting at their desks trying to get their start-ups off the ground. Instead of staring at the wall and wondering what they have got themselves into, they can look at my mug while drinking tea and remind themselves who they are – and that what they are doing is worthwhile.

I decide that the writing will go all the way round the mug because a) it will look different from every other mug out there, and b) as a left-hander I am fed up with mugs which have designs on just one side which only face outwards if a right-handed person is using them.

And I don't have to stop at mugs. I can make a whole range of inspiring products with the word ENTREPRENEUR written on them to support and encourage budding entrepreneurs.

As soon as my friend and his girlfriend have left I turn on the computer and start calculating how much my mugs would cost to make and whether I could sell them for enough margin to make my business work. I already know of a small British business which prints mugs and they helpfully list prices for different quantities ordered on their website. After doing some scribbled calculations on the back of an envelope – yes, literally, and I didn't even realise I was doing it – I decide the answer is, yes, it could work, just about.

Then I buy the domain names entrepreneurmugs.com and entrepreneurmugs.co.uk and feel proud of myself for being so restrained. Entrepreneur mugs. Just perfect. I go to bed full of thoughts and plans.

The next morning I wake up early and decide that entrepreneurmugs.com is a silly name. Not only it is too restricting for my potentially vast business empire, I'm now thinking it could also be seen as rather insulting, implying either that entrepreneurs are mugs or that people who buy my mugs are mugs. Ah well, easily fixed. After a few more hours glued to Lowcostnames.co.uk, trying and failing to buy entrepreneurstuff, entrepreneurkit, entrepreneurgear and a dozen more alternatives, I manage to buy entrepreneurthings.co.uk and entrepreneurthings.com. Job done.

ACTION PLAN

▶▶ Write down a list of possible business ideas to pursue. Then write down a list of pros and cons next to each one.

▶▶ Spend a morning imagining you are a customer for the products or services you plan to sell. Where would you go and buy them at the moment? How would your business be able to do it better? And bearing in mind that people are generally resistant to change, what would entice customers to switch to buying from you?

▶▶ Always buy both dot com and dot co.uk endings for your domains names even if you don't think you need them. One day you will need them, and at the very least it stops anyone else buying them and either trading off or wrecking the reputation you have established.

CHAPTER 4

HOW TO SPEND NOTHING ON PREMISES

Guess how much Richard Powell spends on running the head office at his consulting firm Crimson and Co. each year. £100,000? £200,000? £500,000? Remember the final bill will not just be for the cost of renting the office, it will also need to include business rates and the cost of paying for lighting, heating, reception staff, cleaning, maintenance and so on. Made your guess yet?

Well, the answer is zero. That's right. Nothing. That's because even though Richard's firm now employs thirty staff and has a turnover of £4 million, it doesn't actually have a head office. Or, indeed, any kind of office. Instead all the employees work from home and in the offices of their clients. Then they all meet once a month for a catch-up in a serviced office which has been rented for the day. So rather than having to foot the bill for a huge set of fixed costs each month, Richard only has to pay for the cost of hiring the serviced offices one day a month, plus the cost of travel for his employees – a fraction of what it would cost him to maintain a permanent head office.

Richard says he decided to do away with having a head office after working for big consultancies which maintained huge premises – which none of its employees ever used, because whenever they were hired for a project they would work at the clients' offices instead.

He says: 'I would turn up and nobody would be there apart from a secretary.'

For him there are other benefits, too – the ability to employ the best person for a job, no matter where they live in the country; the fantastic team spirit that meeting up once a month has fostered; and the fact that not paying for an office means he can charge clients less and so undercut the competition.

Location, location, location

So where are you going to run your business? When you are just starting out it makes sense to base yourself at home, but the chances are you are also going to need somewhere to hold meetings, or to store things, or simply to sell your product or service direct to customers. The good news is there are lots of free or nearly free options.

Let's start with meetings. When Richard Powell and his two business partners first started up Crimson and Co., the three of them would meet every few weeks in the lobby of a hotel at Birmingham airport to swap notes, because it was halfway between Richard's home in Chester and where the other two lived in Berkshire. Absolutely no cost involved, apart from the petrol and the coffee.

Hotel lobbies can be good, cheap places to hold meetings. They are classier than Starbucks and for nothing more than the price of coffee you can hold a meeting in the plush surroundings of the lobby or lounge. Indeed, for the price of two or three coffees drunk very slowly, you can spend an entire day there holding meetings. It's warm, it's smart, there is probably free wifi: what's not to love?

The hotels are happy with this arrangement, too, because although you are not spending much, you are bringing life to their communal spaces which in turn makes it more attractive to other people who might think about ordering lunch.

A word of warning, though – you must never forget you are still in a public place. Other people can see who you are meeting, and they can hear your phone calls. I was in a café recently and I could hear the woman at the next table telling someone on the phone all sorts of confidential details about her business, which she had recently sold. You can never be too careful about who might be listening in.

You also need to think about who you are meeting and why. If you are running a recruitment firm and need to interview candidates, for example, they are going to expect – and require – total privacy. They are not going to take kindly to being interviewed in a public place, where everyone can see them, and where anyone can potentially overhear private information. Not only that, but putting someone in that position is going to make you and your business look really unprofessional. Hire a conference room or hotel suite for the day and do the job properly.

But what if you need a space where customers can come and buy your products? There are lots of free options here, too. In fact you can literally start with your home. House parties can be a brilliant way of getting your product or service in front of potential customers, and right now they are enjoying a renaissance. Forget Tupperware parties; these days enterprising entrepreneurs are using their homes to sell everything from children's clothes to jewellery. All you need is a big enough house and lots of mugs and biscuits. Set the date, invite your friends, get them to invite their friends too and put the kettle on.

Even better, why not invite a couple of other entrepreneurs with products which fit well with yours to come along and sell their stuff at the same time. That way you will attract all their friends and customers as well, and you can all benefit from the buzz of having a lot of potential customers coming through the door.

Go pop-up

If your house isn't big enough then get a friend to play host. Or, failing that, borrow any kind of usable space and call it a pop-up shop. Pop-up shops are basically temporary shops which can be set up in any kind of empty space for a day, a few days or a few weeks. They were once used largely by traders to sell seasonal goods, or by wholesalers to offload excess stock. But they are madly fashionable right now, which is fantastic news for fledgling entrepreneurs as they are a great way to test new products, try out new geographical areas and promote their existing ventures in a low-cost, low-risk way. They are also the ideal way for a business without any money to get off the ground.

There are two main types of pop-up shop – those held in empty retail premises, and those in non-traditional venues, which can be anything from a village hall or a garage to an artist's studio. Depending on how much effort you want to put into it, the shop space can be transformed with temporary fittings, or left bare apart from rails and racks on which to display the goods for sale. Either way, the idea – and the big appeal – is that they are not around for long, from a day to several weeks; a season at most. That gives the venture an element of surprise and one of urgency – what does it sell? I'd better go and check it out before it disappears – both of which are likely to appeal to customers looking for something new and different.

When Mary McDermott, whose business We Make London sells jewellery and handbags handmade by British designers, opened her first pop-up shop in an artist's studio in Hampstead, she had no idea what kind of reaction it would get. After fitting the studio out with temporary fixtures and fittings she opened the shop for just eight days – and was astonished to take £10,000 in sales in that time, far more than she would ever have imagined. Unsurprisingly, she is now planning to do more.

She says: 'It was really successful. People were coming in

and saying, "ooh, this looks different". It was definitely a draw for people in the area.'

The other benefit of both pop-up shops and house sales is that they enable you to get instant customer reaction to what you are selling – talk to the people browsing your products and you will soon discover why they like them, or indeed why they don't. Are they too expensive? Or too flimsy? Are the colours weird or the sizes wrong? You will very quickly find out.

Kate Ward and her sister Sarah Loader have found the idea of temporary venues so appealing that they have swapped their bricks and mortar tea shop for a pop-up version. The pair used to run The Silver Apples, a vintage tea room in West Didsbury, Manchester. But after three years they were so fed up with seeing their profits being eaten up by rent and rates that they closed their doors and hit the road with a pop-up version of their tea room.

Their temporary tea room can be created in both indoor and outdoor spaces and the two of them go to great lengths to make it look exactly like a proper traditional English tea room, bringing tables, chairs, a counter, cake stands, linen and vintage crockery with them to decorate the space. They play period music on a record player and to complete the look the sisters, who do the waitressing, wear old-fashioned tea dresses.

Kate says: 'We can really transform a space and make it look gorgeous, and that is what we like about it. People love it because it looks like a proper tea room. They like the thought that has gone into it to make it nice for them.'

Now every weekend the sisters load up their van and head

for venues such as the market hall in Altrincham, Cheshire, where they create their tea room for the monthly vintage fair. Customers can find out where they will be next by checking their website. The tea room also promotes the sisters' catering company, which makes the cakes they serve, and they do not intend ever to go back to permanent premises.

Embrace the concept

Another great way of selling your products in a retail environment without having to open a shop yourself is to take space in a 'concept' store – a communal retail space which sells a mix of brands, products and services provided by a range of small local businesses.

There are two big advantages to selling in a concept store. The first is that there are no upfront charges or overheads, or even rent – you simply display your products in the store for free and the owner of the store takes a percentage of the retail price of everything you sell. It means you get to sell your products in a retail environment, but without the huge financial commitment of renting your own shop on the high street.

The second advantage of this arrangement is that you don't actually have to be there yourself selling your products. The concept store employs its own staff at the tills, where bar codes determine which of your products have been sold and therefore what you are owed. Which means you can be off growing your business elsewhere while your products are flying off the shelves in the communal space.

This is exactly what Azita Yorrick has done. She has started her own venture, Nancy Leigh Knit, making hand-knitted scarves, hats and mittens for adults and children, and selling merino wool in a range of colours. She began by selling her products on a stall in East Dulwich market in south London every Saturday. Sometimes she would take very little in a day, sometimes she would take a lot, but either way she would have to be there in person, standing behind her stall from dawn till dusk.

But now she has discovered Ed Warehouse in East Dulwich, a refurbished Victorian warehouse with a gallery and café which is home to a range of boutique shops and services. It sells everything from fashion and furniture to jewellery and homeware, and Azita and her friend Julia Knight, who runs a business called Recycled Beauty, have taken a space in one corner to create a haberdashery department, selling Azita's wool and Julia's sewing thread, buttons and needles. The products are displayed on an old sideboard which the two have brought into the warehouse, and Azita plans to sell her finished garments there, too. They don't pay anything for the space – the warehouse owner simply takes a 33 per cent cut of everything that is sold. The only commitment from Azita is that she has agreed not to sell her wool anywhere else in East Dulwich other than on her market stall.

She says: 'Spending Saturdays on the market stall is a hard old slog so it's really nice to have somewhere where my wool can be sold without me actually having to be there.'

If you need a selling space which is more permanent, but not overwhelmingly so, then you have also chosen a good time to go about it. Business closures and the poor economic climate have left landlords scrambling to fill their vacant shops, and, on top of that, new laws requiring landlords to pay business rates on empty property have meant they are likely to look much more favourably on the idea of a temporary lodger.

This means that whereas in the past landlords would have normally demanded a five- or ten-year lease, many are now happy to offer short-term leases of two years or less, often at big rent reductions. They are prepared to do this because accepting a low rent for a short time will not affect their property values, which are determined by rental yield. And because it means their property will at least be filled and earning them some income rather than standing empty.

Meanwhile, the small enterprise gets reduced rent and a chance to try out their idea in a prime retail location for a season, or for six months, or a year, without having to commit to an expensive and restrictive long-term lease.

Be co-operative

If the word co-operative makes you think of woolly jumpers and endless inconclusive meetings, then think again. The past few years have seen a surge in the number of co-operatives which have been formed by entrepreneurs and small start-ups with the aim of cutting overheads by sharing rent, equipment and expertise.

Known as co-operative consortia, they work in the same egalitarian way as other co-ops, such as housing and community groups, with all members sharing the benefits, but the emphasis is squarely on the bottom line.

There are now almost 1,000 co-operative consortia in the UK in all sectors – from manufacturing to website design and from farmers to consultants.

The Open Space co-operative in Manchester, for example, was set up by six individuals who wanted a better deal on renting offices. Since 2008 the members, including a web designer, an online marketing company and a political cartoonist, have been renting a former workshop in Hulme and each paying only £100 a month for a desk with a telephone and internet access. The group, which has grown to twelve people, has also discovered the benefits of sharing skills.

Finn Lewis, one of the founders, who runs a web design firm, says: 'The great thing about being a co-operative is that we are our own landlords, but over the past eighteen months all sorts of other benefits that we weren't expecting have come to light. The marketing guy advises us and we advise other people about their websites. The amount of knowledge in there is incredible.'

It is not just premises which can be shared. In return for a £50–£100 annual fee, members of the Forest of Avon Products co-operative benefit from a website and promotional activities such as stands at trade fairs. The Bristol-based co-op also has a wood yard with eight workshops which it rents at below market rate to the forty-five members, which include furniture makers, playground equipment manufacturers and charcoal suppliers.

Skills and equipment are shared, as is work, with the

more established members often passing work to the smaller sole traders.

Self-storage is not just for storing

But what if you simply need more space? When Roger Macdonald and Helen Archer started up an online business selling party decorations, Part Eaz, they quickly ran out of room at home to store their stock. The venture was, however, still far too small to justify renting a warehouse with all the costs that would entail. So they came up with an ingenious solution – renting a self-storage unit and running their operation from there. They now rent 600 sq ft at their local Big Yellow Self Storage in Southend for £315 a month.

It is not hard to see the appeal. As Roger says: 'We have to pay only one cost per month – our rental fee. We don't incur council rates, water charges, electricity charges or any other amenity costs that come with running a business.'

The original purpose of self-storage units, such as those run by Access or Big Yellow Self Storage, was to provide a temporary space to store stuff you can't fit into your house but don't feel quite ready to chuck away. However, a growing number of inventive entrepreneurs have discovered that self-storage units are also great places from which to run a small business. Because if you look at it the other way round, they also function really well as mini pay-as-you-go warehouses.

With significant advantages, too. There is no need to become locked into a long-term rental agreement and there is round-the-clock security and often 24-hour access – ideal for fledgling entrepreneurs trying to juggle a day job with their new venture. There are trolleys on hand to move stock around and deliveries can be left in reception.

Indeed, in response to demand from small businesses, some self-storage operators have begun to provide offices to rent by the month on the same sites as their storage units too. Access, for example, has fifty-three sites around the country which offer both units and offices. Offices can be rented from a minimum of one month and the price includes business rates, heating, lighting and service charges.

Chris Beattie runs his environmentally friendly courier service, WEGO Couriers, from an Access self-storage unit in the centre of Nottingham. He rents a 200 sq ft unit on the ground floor to store his bikes and has a separate space upstairs which he uses as an office for the business, which has a turnover of £250,000 a year.

He says: 'Using a storage unit is very flexible. You are not restricted to three-year contracts and you can add more space when you want. They have a forklift truck, which is great because it means I don't have to train staff, and all the health and safety of the building is managed by them. There are security cameras everywhere and they are monitored twenty-four hours a day.'

Access says that more than 90 per cent of the units at some sites are now being used by businesses, ranging from fine-art dealers and champagne merchants to taxi companies and plumbers.

Rental costs vary according to size and location and the set-up works best for wholesale and online businesses – retailers are not permitted to trade from the sites. Storage sizes range from a lock-up box the size of a washing machine to a 5,000 sq ft warehouse.

Hanging on the telephone

If your venture doesn't actually need an office or storage space, just someone to answer the phone, then all you need is an answering service to do it on your behalf. They are a great low-cost alternative to hiring a real receptionist and installing him or her in a real office, and they give a much better impression than you wheezing down the phone while running for a bus.

You do have to get it right, however, otherwise you will infuriate more customers than you impress. My friend Jane runs a small business and because she never, ever answers her phone she has started employing the services of a virtual receptionist to do it for her. The problem is she has instructed the woman answering the phone to say, 'I'm sorry but Jane is on another call at the moment.'

It doesn't matter how many hundreds of times you phone, Jane will always be 'on another call'. Which is utterly infuriating. In fact, I just tried her number now, twice, to make sure I hadn't dreamed the whole thing up, and, yes, there was the lady, saying, 'I'm afraid she's on another call at the moment.' The second time I called, the lady even put me on hold while she pretended to check if Jane was free, but, sure enough, within a few seconds she had come back to me saying she was sorry but Jane was on another call.

Sometimes I feel like saying, very politely, I know she isn't really on another call, in fact she's not even in the building, because she hasn't actually got a building, and right now she's probably miles away in a meeting, or in the gym, or whatever. Please can't we give up this pretence and accept that she's just not there?

In fact, I actually did say all that once. It didn't make any difference of course. The pleasant voiced woman continued to insist that Jane was on another call at the moment, and I hung up.

Remember, first impressions count – a lot – and you need to consider the impression you give, whether deliberately or inadvertently, to your customers. If you don't get it right the first time you may not be given a second chance.

ACTION PLAN

▶▶ Think about what kind of space your
customers are going to feel comfortable in
– do they need privacy? Or accessibility? Or
a congenial atmosphere?

▶▶ If possible make sure your space will be
able to grow with your business, at least
for the first few years. It will be a lot less
disruptive that way.

▶▶ Put yourself in your customers' shoes and
try out your own answering service. If you
are happy with it, great. If not, change it.

CHAPTER 5

HOW TO SPEND NOTHING ON STAFF

As a child, Tarek Nseir loved taking things apart – toasters, telephones, anything he could get his hands on – to find out how they worked. When he was fourteen his mother, who ran a business providing security services, bought an Amstrad computer which Tarek learnt to use. Soon he was earning pocket money by helping her and her clients with their computers, installing software and setting up servers. So when he was in his first year at Newcastle University studying information systems, Tarek decided to pitch for a £20,000 contract to design the website of a trade organisation, the Minor Metal Trades Association, for whom he had already installed a computer system.

There was just one problem. He had no design skills and no money. Undaunted, he put up posters at Northumbria University, which was just across the road and had a creative department, asking for designers at £30 an hour. By the time he got back to his room a few hours later there was a queue of fourteen students keen to be taken on. There was, however, a catch. Tarek says: 'They sat in my lounge and I dropped the bombshell that I wouldn't be able to pay them unless we won the contract.'

Nevertheless, three of the fourteen students stuck with Tarek. The team won the pitch for the work and designed the website together. At the end of the job he paid them all the money they had earned at a rate of £30 an hour, as promised, and still walked away with a profit of £12,000 for himself. What's more, one of the three students, Gary Glozier, continued to work with Tarek on other projects and is now the co-founder and creative director of Tarek's firm, Think, a design agency which has a turnover of £11 million. Clients include J. K. Rowling's Harry Potter website, Pottermore, as well as Sony, the BBC and Lloyds TSB.

If you need staff to help you run your business and you don't have any money, there is a simple solution: hire them for specific projects on a freelance basis and then arrange to pay them – with their agreement – only when your business has received payment from the end client. That way you can access all the specialist help you need without having to finance the cost by other means.

There is a double benefit to hiring freelance workers as and when you need them on specific projects: not only do you pay only for the help you need, you also get access to highly skilled workers who might not actually want, or be able, to work for your fledgling enterprise full-time.

Professionals who may have balked at the idea of working solely for a small start-up are likely to be more than happy to provide their services for a day a week or two days a month, for example.

The good news is that the opportunities to hire people for specific projects have expanded dramatically in the past few years. There are now some really useful websites which have been specifically created to bring together small firms looking for talent, and skilled professional workers looking for work on a freelance basis. Some sites are focused on design; others offer contractors who can work in a wide range of areas. The sites are generally free for businesses to register – they only pay for the work done.

The website 99designs.co.uk, for example, connects designers from around the world with customers seeking affordable designs for things such as logos, websites and brochures. The customer, i.e. the entrepreneur, submits a design brief. Freelance designers then compete for the job, and the customer chooses which one they like best. They receive the final design along with the copyright of the original artwork. Costs range from £125 for a business card or letterhead to £195 for a logo.

Another website, Concept Cupboard (conceptcupboard. com), brings together creative graduates and firms looking for someone to carry out a specific project, for example designing a logo or website.

Odesk (odesk.com) has a wider brief, providing contractors of all kinds who can be hired for specific projects in areas such as sales and marketing, IT or customer services. Customers pay by the hour and the website's online work diary function means the customer can easily verify how much time the contractors are spending on the project, as screenshots and memos are recorded as they work.

Peopleperhour (peopleperhour.com) allows small businesses to hire someone for a few hours a week to work on a specific project, again based on the principle that freelancers bid for the job and the customer awards the work to the one they feel would do the best job.

If you are looking for more general help, consider taking on a recent graduate as an intern for a few weeks. The benefits are twofold: they gain the experience they need to help them stand out from the crowd in the job market; you gain an intelligent pair of hands for little cost. Several websites have been set up to match small businesses and graduate interns, such as Enternships (enternships.com) and Inspiring Interns (inspiringinterns.com). Do always pay expenses and at least a small wage, though.

Another option is simply to ask your mum to help. When Andrew Dunn started his skiing holiday operation, Scott Dunn, he managed to persuade his mother, Joan, to do all the administration for his fledgling company from the spare bedroom of her home in Hampshire. She would take bookings by phone while Andrew stayed out in Champéry in the Swiss Alps where he had hired a couple of chalets, to look after the business on the ground.

He says: 'She did a great job running the business with one of those green Amstrad computers. I utterly trusted her and she is a people person so she was great at getting the bookings. She worried terribly when we had empty beds. She was just fantastic.'

His mother ended up working for him for two years on an unpaid basis until the business could afford to hire someone else to do the administration. Andrew later gave her a 1 per cent equity stake to say thank you.

That early support was invaluable. Scott Dunn Travel now employs 280 people worldwide and has a turnover of £27 million.

When Vicki Snow asked her mother to run the office of her public relations company, Snow PR, she was worried what the other people working for her would think. She needn't have. They feel so comfortable with her mother that they often go to her with their problems.

'I was not sure how people would react to me having my mum here; whether they felt they could talk properly in front of her when I wasn't in the office,' says Vicki, who now employs ten people at her fashion and retail PR firm in London's West End. 'But all the girls love her. When they need help they run to Mum.'

Her mother, Christine Robinson, now works two days a week for the business. Vicki says: 'I trust and rely on her 100 per cent. It has been hugely supportive having her here. I love the fact that Mum is part of what I am doing.'

Her mother is happy too, saying: 'I love the industry and the atmosphere in the office is fantastic.'

Getting your mother – or, indeed, your father – to help you out while you get the business off the ground will not work for everyone, however. For a start, if you are one of those people who instantly reverts back to thinking and acting like an eight-year-old whenever their parents are around, it is clearly not going to work.

And second, asking someone to make the leap from family member to employee is a big request, particularly if they are only doing it to help you out and would really much rather be spending their days playing golf or bridge. What happens if they make a mistake and get something wrong? What happens if they start doing things differently from how you would like?

If you do get your mum or dad to help you:

▶▶ Set the ground rules so you both know what they are supposed to be doing – and for how long

▶▶ Don't get cross if they do it wrong – remember they are helping you out as a labour of love

▶▶ Reward them when the business takes off. Everyone likes to be appreciated

The magic of outsourcing

The key idea to remember when starting a business without any money is the importance of choosing variable costs over fixed costs; in other words, only paying for goods and services as and when you need them. The best way to do that is by outsourcing all the functions of your operation.

From the outside, Frank & Faith looks like a business which employs a lot of staff. It sells ethical fashion and homewear through its website and exports to ten countries.

In fact, until recently the company had just one employee:

its founder, Anya Pearson. The manufacturing, marketing and website design are all outsourced, with the clothes made in three factories in the Midlands. So, as it grows, Frank & Faith is creating jobs not at the firm itself but at the factories and manufacturers which supply it.

'This way I am able to tap into the skills and expertise of the people working at the factories,' says Anya, who ran Frank & Faith from her home near Dorchester, Dorset, until she successfully sold it for a substantial undisclosed sum in 2011.

The different perspective that comes from outsourcing is a great advantage for a small enterprise. 'You can get a bit stuck in a rut and bogged down in your own world,' Anya says. 'The person who manages our website is able to come to it with fresh eyes and keep it looking modern because she is separate from the business.'

The model has clearly worked well – Anya sold Frank & Faith just five years after starting it when a potential investor, one of the biggest online ethical retailers in the UK, decided they liked the company so much they wanted to acquire it in its entirety rather than just a chunk. Anya is now planning a new business venture.

These days virtually every element of business can be outsourced, from administration, accounting, sales, marketing and manufacturing to web design and development.

Dave Willis was working as a distributor of snacks and crisps to pubs when the launch of a new brand of hand-cooked crisps, Burts Chips, forced him to rethink. He called Burts to ask if he could be a distributor for their crisps, too, but when they told him they would be doing it themselves

Dave realised that the crisps he was selling would not be strong enough to compete against the newcomer. He decided that the way forward lay in making his own brand of crisps rather than simply selling other people's. He did not have enough money to start a manufacturing operation of his own so he found a local factory with spare capacity to make the crisps for him, to his specifications, and asked his sister, a packaging designer, to design the packets. He called his crisps Salty Dog. The crisps went on sale in 2003 and today 10 million bags a year are sold in 16 countries, producing a turnover of £3 million.

Indeed, outsourcing means that companies can now grow to quite a substantial size while continuing to employ only one person – the founder. In a survey of home businesses which expected to increase their turnover, half planned to do so by outsourcing or using freelancers, according to Enterprise Nation, the home business network. Only 4 per cent planned to expand by hiring full-time staff.

Penny Power co-founded Ecademy, a social networking site for small businesses, in 2000. The ability to outsource has transformed the way she runs the operation. Even though it has grown to a turnover of £1 million, her venture, which is based in Surrey, still has only two employees in addition to its three founders.

'There is no way our business would have existed if we had had the overheads and the risk of people working for us,' says Penny. 'In the early days we didn't need a full-time finance person, we needed a book-keeper who did ten hours a week and an accountant once a month. Outsourcing allows you to find good people and pay them only when you need them.'

Do protect your business

Paul Morris grew up in Stafford wanting to be a vet; when he failed to get the necessary qualifications he went to work for a chemicals company which sold colour additives for polymers and then moved to an additives manufacturer which made performance substances such as UV stabilisers. While he was there he developed a range of antimicrobial additives which could be added to plastic products such as chopping boards and kitchen equipment and so prevent bacteria from growing on them, thereby reducing the spread of germs.

But when his wife, who worked as a psychologist in intensive care at Stafford hospital, told him about the dangers of MRSA, Paul realised there was a real need for antimicrobial products in hospitals, too, which would be resistant to bacteria and so help prevent cross-infection. Paul suggested the idea to his boss but he was noncommittal – and when his boss also refused to give Paul an equity stake in the firm, Paul quit at the age of thirty to develop antimicrobial products himself.

It was a risky move since his wife was seven months pregnant with their first child. Paul started the business with £5,000 given to him by his grandmother. He began experimenting by adding silver, known for its antimicrobial properties, to materials such as plastics, paper and paint and discovered it worked well in stopping the growth of bacteria on them.

From the start Paul chose not to have his own laboratory or manufacturing plant, preferring to outsource the testing and production to local manufacturers.

He says: 'I am a big believer in outsourcing. I think if someone does the job better than you, and you can switch them on and off as you need them, that is a strength, not a weakness.'

Four months after starting out, he sold his first antimicrobial additive to a firm making nappy bags. Called Biomaster, it is now added to many products used in hospitals such as paint, handrails, light switches and doctors' case note folders.

But Paul also learnt – the hard way – one extremely important lesson about outsourcing: you need to fiercely protect the knowledge you are sharing with others. When he started the business in 2000 Paul asked all his manufacturers to sign three-year confidentiality agreements. But when the agreements ran out one manufacturer refused to re-sign. Paul soon discovered that the manufacturer was making similar products and offering them to its customers at a lower price.

Paul says, with some understatement: 'It was very messy for six months.'

Fortunately he managed to persuade his customers to stick with him, not least because if they had chosen to go elsewhere for cheaper products they would have missed out on any future products he was developing. He now insists that all manufacturers sign rolling agreements which run indefinitely. His firm, which is based in Stafford, now has a turnover of £3 million.

If you are going to outsource, make sure you are completely protecting the information you share – with detailed confidentiality agreements, otherwise known as non-disclosure agreements, backed by stiff penalties. The Intellectual

Property Office (ipo.gov.uk) provides free templates for non-disclosure agreements on its website. The agreement is a legally binding document – both parties simply need to sign and date it and each should retain a copy.

Above all, though, make sure you stay in constant and personal touch with the firms doing work for you. That way you will immediately be able to sense if something is not quite right. The personal relationship is every bit as important as the business relationship, and you need to nurture both.

ACTION PLAN

▶▶ Define the role or function you need to fill as precisely as possible to get the best fit.

▶▶ Along with members of your family, students are another useful, untapped resource. Get in touch with your local college or university – if you have a relevant and interesting project they might even be able to work on it as part of their course.

▶▶ Draw up a confidentiality agreement for every project and every person, whether they are part-time book-keeper, outsourced designer creating a logo or expenses-only intern. Make sure it is signed and up to date.

CHAPTER 6

TAKING THE NEXT STEP

On with my fledgling business. The mug-printing firm I found sells all shapes and sizes of mugs, and after studying their website I choose a ceramic mug with a shape known as Durham (all mug shapes have different names, quite a few of them named after British towns for some reason). Then I call them to discuss my plans and instantly I'm faced with a dilemma. I want to buy from a British firm because I think it is important to champion and support home-grown enterprises where possible. But although the firm is British and based in Preston, it doesn't actually make the mugs itself. Like virtually all mug-printing operations in the UK, it imports the plain mugs from Thailand and China and then adds the designs to them in its factory in Liverpool. Does that still count as a British-made mug if the designs are added on in Liverpool? Well, yes and no, I guess.

The mug firm does actually supply an entirely British-made mug, which is made in Stoke-on-Trent, the traditional home of pottery making. In theory this would be the perfect solution. In theory. The problem is, I don't actually like that mug: to me it looks really old-fashioned with its sticky out lip at the top and the curly ear-shaped handle. It is every mug you have ever been given as a free promotional gift and immediately relegated to the back of the cupboard so no one can see it.

On the other hand the Durham mug, the one made in Thailand and China, is gorgeous, with its straight sides and perfectly shaped D handle. Everyone will want to buy my mugs if they look like this; equally, no one will want to buy them if I choose the British mug, and I won't have a business. It's the classic dilemma that so many firms have to make on a daily basis. What to do?

I choose the Durham mug but promise myself that if sales volumes get high enough to justify it, I will go direct to the British mug factory in Stoke-on-Trent and ask them to make some British-made Durham mugs just for me. A total cop-out or a sensible commercial decision? You decide.

And so to the design. After much happy playing about with the paint programme on my computer, I come up with a simple but effective design for my mugs. Big bold capital letters on a plain colour background which runs right round the mug from one side of the handle to the other.

After the design, the next important decision to make is the colour. Colour is incredibly important in branding – you only have to think of the red of Virgin Atlantic and Coca-Cola, or the orange of EasyJet. They not only make the company brand stand out, they are also such instantly recognisable colours that you could probably guess which company they represented purely from the colour alone. So I really need to select something which will look professional as well as inspirational.

I create twenty-five different colour combinations on my computer and line them all up next to each other. That way I can see what my options are and make the best decision. It may seem time-consuming but, whatever your own product or service, make sure you have thoroughly researched all possible options before making your decision. A wrong step now could cost dearly later on.

I choose two alternative colour schemes – orange on blue and purple on green – and order sample mugs to see what they look like for real. Unfortunately I have chosen badly. Orange on blue and purple on green may look fabulous on a computer screen but it looks much less fabulous on a real-life 3-D mug. Good job I only ordered samples.

The next design is much more successful because a) I've decided to ask the advice of Denis the designer at the mug firm, who b) thinks that a single-colour background with white writing on it will work better. He's right, it does. Less really is more, in this case. After much staring at colour charts I choose a deep pink and a dark blue. It will be interesting to see which proves to be more popular with customers. Because these mugs are being printed in a different way from the first design – in order to make the white really white – I can't put the entrepreneurthings.com website address on the base of the mug any more, so we come up with a way of incorporating it into the design itself by running it up the side of the colour band. The samples arrive and look amazing. Phew.

There is just one more decision to make – whether to get polystyrene boxes or cardboard boxes for packaging the individual mugs. Polystyrene will be better for sending the mugs through the post, cardboard will be better for when people buy mugs from me in person. I order half of each.

The minimum order is for 108 mugs, which with packaging and delivery and VAT comes to a total of £534.86 in total. As I am a new customer with no previous trading history I have to pay this upfront – but fortunately I had anticipated this and so have already taken enough advance orders with payment from friends and family – for fifty-four mugs at £10 each, some people buying several – to cover the upfront cost.

This is a brilliant way of funding your first order, by the way. People who know you are not going to mind waiting a bit longer for their order to arrive, and it is a much more effective way of getting the funding you need than simply asking your friends and family to lend you the money because a) it looks more professional, and b) it means they actually get to own and use your products. If they have bought several of them they might decide to give some to their friends, who in turn might recommend them to their friends, and so the message about your business starts to spread.

Two weeks later, my mugs arrive on the back of a van in three big cardboard boxes. I immediately check them all for quality. It's a good job I do because some of them are damaged – someone at the factory obviously put the mugs into the polystyrene boxes too quickly and so the polystyrene has melted on to the mugs, wrecking both box and mug. I call Denis, who says he will send replacements straight away.

The boxes of mugs block my hall but it doesn't matter. I'm on my way now. In fact in many ways I've just done the hardest bit, because the real challenge of starting a venture is actually taking the first step. You can always make adjustments once you get going.

This is what happened to James Nash. The product which inspired James to start a business has actually ended up being his biggest flop. To date he has sold just four of the bicycle docking stations which he designed while at university to provide a compact way of parking bikes. But the momentum it created has spawned a £3 million business.

James had a prototype of his bicycle docking station made by a welder and attempted to sell the bike dock to councils, hospitals and educational establishments for £3,000 apiece. But after a couple of months of struggling to market the bike dock he realised that unless he found something else to sell, he wouldn't actually have a business. 'I can laugh about it now, but at the time I didn't find it that funny,' he admits.

Instead his firm, Bike Dock Solutions, has ended up making money from selling simpler n-shaped bike stands which are commonly found on urban streets. He and his business partner, Josh Coleman, have also started up two other ventures, one selling street furniture and the other selling upmarket cabins.

Bike Dock Solutions now sells 350 products, including stands, shelters and lockers, and won the Transport for

London tender to provide bike parking for two of the cycle superhighways into London. In total the three businesses turn over £3.4 million and employ fourteen staff.

The first step can be the tiniest, simplest thing to do. It doesn't have to be a grand gesture; it can be very small, no more than a mark in the sand to show your intent. But the first step will inspire the second step, and so on, until your venture takes on a life of its own.

The dull but important stuff

There are three more things I have to do before I can start selling my mugs. I need to open a business bank account, I need to incorporate my company and make it a legal entity, and I need to protect my design.

I decide that opening a bank account will be the easiest so I tackle this first. It's not. My accountant told me that business bank accounts are all pretty much the same and that it was just a matter of picking one. I'm glad I didn't take his advice because once I started looking into it I realised not all bank accounts are created equal. In fact there are huge differences between them which could spell the difference between my bank account costing me nothing to run, and it costing me hundreds of pounds a year.

The first step when you are doing this yourself is to check out how much free banking you will get. The high street banks all try to entice new start-up customers with an initial period of free banking, but how long you get can differ widely. Some banks offer two years' free business banking, for example, some offer eighteen months and some only offer twelve months.

But while this free-banking period is helpful, it is what happens after the free period ends that you really need to consider when selecting a bank. After all, if your venture takes off, you are likely to be with the bank you choose for a long time because the effort involved in switching to another bank will be enormous. Some bank accounts charge a fee for every cheque you pay in, for example, plus a handling fee for cash paid in, so if you are going to be doing this regularly you need an account that allows a certain number of cheques and amount of cash to be paid in without charge each month. On the other hand if you are starting an online venture and customers will mainly pay by credit or debit cards through your website, you need an account which offers free automated transactions. Some offer this, some don't, so check.

Watch out, too, for the monthly service charge. Some banks charge several pounds a month whereas others do not charge a monthly fee at all. A few pounds a month may not sound like a lot, but it adds up – £5 a month, for example, is £300 over five years.

Many banks also try to tempt start-ups to join them by offering software packages or trial offers. These may include free online advice videos from well-known successful entre-preneurs, access to business lounges, or free trials of accounting software.

Beware, however, banks offering expensive start-up pack-ages which may include such things as consultations with an accountant and solicitor, a credit check service, online data back-up and management software. Check that the services offered are actually going to be useful to your business; the higher monthly fee soon adds up so if you don't need them, don't sign up.

You also need to think about what level of personal service you would like from your bank. Some bank accounts are free because all communication with customers is done by email instead of face to face. Alternatively, you may prefer to opt for an account which comes with a dedicated manager who you can meet in person, but which charges a monthly fee for doing so.

Ask if you will have a dedicated relationship manager or simply a team responding to your queries. Then go online and find out what other small-business customers are saying about the bank. If a bank is generating more than its fair share of complaints about its service, it might be wise to avoid it.

Another factor is how quickly you will be able to start using your account. While some banks will have your account up and running at the end of a ninety-minute meeting provided there are no problems with your application, at others you may find yourself having to wait up to ten working days before you can use it.

Also consider where your bank is located, and how many branches it has. When I opened a business bank account I chose between the three close to my home, because I knew I would not want to travel far every time I needed to go into a branch.

Here are the questions you need to ask: how long is the free-banking period? Are there any conditions attached? How long will I have to wait until my bank account is opened? Will I have a dedicated relationship manager? If so, how will I be able to contact him or her? How much does it cost to pay in cheques and cash, and to make automated online payments? Will the account be able to handle foreign currency transactions?

One question I'm often asked by would-be entrepreneurs is why they actually need to open a business bank account. Can't they just use their personal bank account, which does not charge a fee for writing cheques, or paying money in, instead? The answer is no. First, if you try to combine your personal money and your business money in one account you are very quickly going to get into a mess trying to work out which money is for what and who it belongs to.

Second, even if you open two separate accounts, the small print in some banks states that you must not use a personal account for business purposes. If the bank discovers you are, it reserves the right to close the account. Limited companies have to have a business account by law, because they have to inform their bank of who the directors of the company are and file their accounts each year.

Third, it is really not a good look for your business if you are constantly operating in the shadows. If you are running a venture from a personal bank account, for example, you can't put the account in your business name, only your own, so it doesn't look professional either to your customers or your suppliers. Get a business bank account from day one, take advantage of the period of free banking, put the account in your business name, go and meet your relationship person and start off in the right way.

And so to establishing my company. I – and you, too – have two main options: become a sole trader or become a limited liability business. A third option is to create a part-nership. Setting up as a sole trader will cost you nothing, and requires you to do no more than register with the government tax office, HMRC (hmrc.gov.uk), for tax and national insurance purposes. The advantage of being a sole trader is that it is quick and easy and simple, but the big disadvantage is you have unlimited personal liability for the debts of your business if something goes wrong. It might also ultimately make your enterprise more difficult to sell if you are a sole trader.

In a partnership, the partners share the risks, costs and responsibilities of being in business between them. The best option if you are planning to build something of substance is to create a limited company, which means your business becomes a separate legal entity and therefore you have limited liability for any debts incurred. If you take this route you will need to incorporate your business as a limited company and register it at Companies House (companie-shouse.co.uk), as well as register with HMRC for tax and national insurance payments.

These days you can incorporate your business online, for example at Efaze (efaze.com), but, if you are worried about doing it yourself or making a mistake, an accountant will do it for you for a small fee. Whichever option you take, when choosing a business name make sure you get one for which you can get the website address too, so that they match. You can check out the names which are already taken by looking on the Companies House website.

Finally, my design needs protecting. It is automatically protected by copyright simply by existing – no one is allowed to take my designs and make their own entrepreneur mugs using them. But I also need to trademark the design by applying for a trademark through the Intellectual Property Office (ipo.gov.uk). It costs £170 to do this online, plus a further £50 for each additional product class. Expensive, but well worth doing.

My mugs are still quite vulnerable to copycats, however – while this will stop other people producing a mug which looks identical, it will not prevent them from producing a similar one in a slightly different design. To protect your own product, make sure the design has something unique to you about it – design your own font, or your own colour, and include something special in the design. Something as simple as putting a star instead of the Es in ENTREPRENEUR, for example, would mark the design out as distinctly mine, rather than just a word.

ACTION PLAN

▶▶ Forget about doing things perfectly. Just take the first step. You can refine things later.

▶▶ Book an appointment at three local banks to discuss opening an account with them and take a list of questions to ask. You will come away with a very strong feeling about which one you want to bank with.

▶▶ If you think your business will have a turnover which takes it above the VAT threshold as set by HMRC – currently £77,000 a year – you will need to register for VAT. You can do this by filling in a form online at the HMRC website.

CHAPTER 7

HOW TO SPEND NOTHING ON A WEBSITE

So you've got your product sorted, you know how to get it to your customers and you know how to get the money rolling in. Now you need a website.

And before you ask, yes, you are definitely going to need a website, regardless of whether your venture is predominantly online or an on-the-ground one. These days a business is invisible without a website. Customers expect one, so you have to have one. It is effectively your shop window to the world explaining what you do and how you do it and will often be the first impression that a new customer has of your business. So it needs to look professional, and it needs to work properly.

Let's look at how you might go about getting one.

You can build a website for free yourself

There are several DIY web builder sites – Moonfruit.com, Basekit.com and Wix.com being three – which provide the templates on their own websites for you to create yourself a free website. They will also host your website for free. (Sites such as these make their money by also offering a range of more advanced options – more pages, more bandwidth, more file storage and so on – which customers pay for by the month. Still a low-cost option and useful to expand into as your business grows.) You can also take a course to learn how to build a website from scratch. A quick search on Floodlight, the online adult course finder, shows that there are 1,052 courses on web design in London alone. Or there are services such as Decoded (decoded.co.uk) which will teach you how to write computer code so you can build one from first principles.

But – and it's a big but – just because you could theoretically build a website for free, it doesn't necessarily mean you should go down that route. It depends what you need your website to be able to do. There is a big difference between creating a website which is basically an information point showing phone numbers and location, and one which enables people to buy things through the site, or requires a complex search function, or social networking functions, or the ability to play videos, or whatever.

Whenever I suggest that individuals might be better off paying an expert to create a website for them rather than battling away trying to do it on their own, I get lots of irate emails from people telling me how easy it was for them to do and that I really should be telling people to create their own for nothing. But the fact is, some of us are technically minded and some of us aren't: if it is going to take you three weeks of pain and sleepless nights, only to end up with some substandard website which doesn't work properly and looks terrible, then you would be better off paying someone else to do it in a fraction of the time and sparing yourself the pain, while you get on with something you are good at. And it is not just about the time saved and pain avoided – if your amateurish website can't process payments properly or if it crashes the moment more than one customer tries to use it, then you are going to lose sales, too. And annoy your customers, who might think twice about returning.

Take me. I decided that if I was going to mention web-building sites as a way of getting a free website then I really should try and create my Entrepreneur Things website on one. The idea is that you click on the design you like, put your own content on it, and then launch your website on their server. There are various levels of functionality, depending on what you require – the most basic free version gives you 20MB of storage, up to fifteen pages, and the option of an online shop.

Well, I managed to register and I managed to click on the design template I wanted. And then I got stuck. I could work out how to delete the dummy text, but I couldn't work out how to write in new text of my own or add pictures. In fact, I still can't. And as I couldn't find instruction manual or helpline number to call, I struggled on for a while, and then I gave up.

And then I realised that if I was actually going to have a website, I was going to need to get someone else to do it for me. So that's what I did. And if you are not the sort of person who can get their head around creating a website, that is what you should do, too. If there is one thing I have learnt from successful entrepreneurs, it is to do the things you are good at, and to get someone else to do the things you are not good at.

The big question is, how to pay for it? Websites cost a lot of money, right? Well, yes and no. There are a number of options:

Paying for it with equity

I run occasional workshops for budding entrepreneurs, and one of the questions guaranteed to produce heated debate every time is whether you should give away equity in your venture in return for getting someone to make you a website. On the one hand you get a lovely website 'for free' instead of having to fork out thousands of pounds upfront – and on the other hand, you don't, because that 'free' equity you happily handed over could turn out to be worth millions one day.

In the course of creating your business there may well be several occasions when you have to think about whether to give away equity in return for something – to secure funding from a private investor, for example, or to attract the services of a brilliant managing director, or even to secure the involvement of a television 'dragon'. But the website question is often the one which catches people out because:

a) it's usually the first 'giving-away equity' decision you have to make;

b) you have to deal with it when you have little or no money and you haven't even got a proper business, so it doesn't really feel as if you are giving away anything of value. People often justify it by pointing out that 10 per cent of nothing is basically nothing anyway. They are wrong – it is not going to feel like nothing when you have to give them 10 per cent of the £20 million you just sold your firm for – but you can see why they might think that way;

c) even though the cost of creating a website has come down a lot in the past couple of years – you can get a website designer to create a fully functioning e-commerce website for between £5,000 and £10,000 – it is still an enormous amount of money if you haven't actually got any.

Rajeeb Dey learnt the hard way about the pros and cons of giving away equity instead of paying for his website upfront. When he started his venture Enternships.com in 2008 to match graduate interns looking for work experience with small firms looking for short-term assistance, he was still a student himself and had no money. So he found a design agency which was willing to design his website in return for a 35 per cent stake.

It didn't take long for Rajeeb to realise he had done a terrible deal. Although he had saved himself the upfront cost of creating the website, he had effectively given away a third of his company for the equivalent of few thousand pounds. Even worse, by taking on a website agency as a partner, as opposed to an individual committing to the project full-time, he quickly discovered that his website was not even their number one priority. The agency had lots of other projects clamouring for attention and so his website suffered endless delays and setbacks as a result. Indeed, it was partly because of the arrangement that the launch of his business was delayed for a year.

Rajeeb says: 'I was completely naive. I didn't understand the value of equity. If I could turn back the clock I wouldn't do it again. I should have borrowed the money from a friend or family and paid someone £5,000–£6,000 to build me a website rather than giving away equity.'

In the end Rajeeb managed to extricate himself from the deal, but only after paying the website design agency thousands of pounds to buy back their stake in the company. He advises now: 'If you are really going to make a go of it you have to think about how valuable your business is going to be in three to five years' time. Don't do what I did. Be really savvy with what you give away.'

Fortunately his venture has since thrived and now has more than 4,000 firms using it to find interns. Enternships. com also has a contract with Santander bank to connect their small and medium-sized customers to students and graduates.

As I still need a website and creating my own is clearly not going to be the most sensible option, it is time for me to work through the whole website payment versus equity dilemma myself.

The first step is to see how much a website designer would charge to create my website. The designer who created my personal website, Rachelbridge.com, offers to do it for £5,000, but I also hear some real horror stories. A friend who wanted to start a business was quoted the astronomical figure of £90,000 by some website designers to create his website; it subsequently emerged they were not even planning to do the work themselves, but to outsource it to cheaper designers overseas. (This, apparently, is increasingly common. Before you part with any cash make sure you ask exactly who is going to be doing the work – and where.)

The next step is to investigate the equity option. So I get in touch with Tim, an old school friend of my sister, who I vaguely remember did something in IT. The good news is that Tim is still in IT, and, even better, he now co-owns a website design agency. Tim says he is happy to design me a website in return for a stake in my fledgling business. Fantastic, I think.

Or, actually, not. Because in the course of our emails to and fro establishing what would be involved, it quickly becomes clear that giving someone a chunk of equity is a lot more complicated than it first seems. There are just so many issues to address and nail down. For example, is the plan that he and his team will simply design a website, or do I – or they – expect them to have a say in how the venture will be run and what direction it will take, too? And how much work should they be expected to do in return for their stake? Will it be a short-term project or will they be on hand to upgrade the site forever? Will they realise their money only if I sell the business? Or will they expect regular dividend payments along the way too? It would be weird, to say the least, if they only work for, say, three months to get the site up and running – and then turn up to collect their £2 million cheque ten years later when I sell up.

I start to raise some of these questions in my emails but we seem to be going round in circles without actually agreeing anything. I begin to feel uneasy. The emails become rather strained. We can't even agree when to reach an agreement – I want to agree everything first before work begins, while Tim wants to do the work first and then make equity decisions based on how much time and effort it has involved. But it is when Tim casually mentions £50,000 as a possible final cost for creating the website that my unease quickly turns to alarm. £50,000? For a basic website selling a mug? Surely that couldn't be right. Yes, I am keen to start on a shoestring – but not if it means digging myself into a future financial black hole. I decide not to pursue our conversation further.

When working through this option yourself, remember that the only possible justification for giving a website designer a stake is if you are expecting the website to need to evolve, perhaps because the market you are entering is new and unformed, and so will need to be continually redesigned and reworked as the market and demand evolves.

Paying for it at the weekend

My third, and as it turned out inspired, option is to find someone who works for an established web design firm, but who is happy to do my website on a freelance basis – with his employer's permission – in the evenings and at weekends. All the skill and knowledge, with all the backup of his employer's firm's resources and troubleshooting to hand, at a fraction of the price. And because he is doing it at weekends it means I can ring him at odd times with queries. Genius. Pete agrees to create for me a fully functioning website for £700, which he accepts on the basis of £350 paid upfront and the rest when I actually start selling mugs. He constructs the website on the Wordpress platform, which means it is easy for me to add more products and pages myself at a later stage. Make sure you do this, too. He initially hosts the website on his own server, and at the end of the project emails me a document containing all the various login details and handing over the intellectual property of the site so that I own it and he doesn't (make sure you also do this, too). And he has given me a full set of instructions so in future I can change the words and pictures without having to ask him all the time. It looks lovely, and it works too.

One thing you are going to have to work out while designing your website is the e-commerce bit – in other words how your customers are going to pay for the products they buy on your website. People going online expect to be able to pay for things using their credit and debit cards, which means you have two basic options. You can either set up a merchant account with the bank where you have your business account, meaning they will process the payments for a fee and put the money into your account, or you can use a bolt-on provider such as PayPal, which will do much the same thing. In the end it comes down to cost and simplicity – while both the bank and PayPal will charge 3 per cent of the cost of each transaction to process it, the bank will also charge a monthly fee and a minimum transaction charge per month, representing an additional minimum cost of £22 per month. Worth it when sales reach a significant level, perhaps, especially as some customers might be a bit wary of using PayPal, but not for the moment. I would also have had to buy, rent or construct a checkout facility for my website. So PayPal it is. Another bank, incidentally, wanted to charge all of the above plus a chunky set-up fee. I started laughing until I realised the lady on the other end of the phone was being serious.

The other thing you need to think about is who is hosting your website. After merrily tweeting about my Entrepreneur Things website and sending out emails to everyone I could think of telling them about it, I receive an email from someone telling me it took her three attempts to get the home page of my Entrepreneur Things website up on her computer screen. And then she could go no further.

On further investigation I discover that most of the time people can't actually access my website at all. Instead, typing in the website address brings up a message saying 'Internal server error 500'. And on the rare occasion they manage to get on to the website, they can't get beyond the home page.

Aarrggh. Everyone knows that if you tell people about a website, they are only going to take a look once, partly out of curiosity but mostly out of politeness so they can say something nice about it the next time they bump into you. If it doesn't work the first time they are very unlikely ever to come back. Which means I have just totally wrecked my very best chance of generating a bit of goodwill towards my tiny venture.

It turns out that the problem is the server. Every website needs to sit on a platform called a server which is supplied by a hosting provider, which, as the term suggests, 'hosts' it and plugs it into the internet in return for a small fee every month. It seems, however, that all servers are not created equal. My website is sitting on Pete's own server, and it is that which is causing the problem because it is not powerful enough to allow access to my website all the time and so is barring people from accessing it for several hours a day. How stupid: what is the point of a website which people can only access sometimes? Anyway, it is clear I need to move my website to a more reliable server. Fast.

Pete emails me: 'This involves finding a hosting package you wish to use, setting that up and then moving the site and databases. You require hosting which supports PHP (Linux Operating System) and MySQL with at least 1GB of storage.'

Great. He might as well have been writing to me in Greek. But he does suggest I check out Go Daddy (godaddy.com), which on its website promises a 99.9 per cent guaranteed uptime. That is more like it.

The Go Daddy website is a technophobe's worst nightmare. Clicking on the hosting options takes me through to a page which offers 'fourth generation hosting' which provides, apparently, 'a completely unique hosting experience'. I scroll down to discover there are three hosting options: economy at a few pounds a month, deluxe at a few more pounds a month, and ultimate at a bit more still a month. All offer unlimited bandwidth and are slightly cheaper if you sign up for 24 or 36 months. I opt for the deluxe version for 24 months. Pete agrees to do the transfer for me, and all is well.

ACTION PLAN

▶▶ Decide whether you want to create your own website or get someone else to do it for you. Then write down what you want your website to do. What functions will it need, both now and later? E-commerce? A blog? Videos? The ability for customers to post reviews? And will designing it be a one-off task or will it need continually to evolve?

▶▶ To find a website designer, go to a free networking event for small businesses being held in your area and ask around for recommendations. Also draw up a list of websites which you like the look of and contact the designer direct – they will have put their name or business at the bottom of the first page.

▶▶ Once your website is up and running, check it constantly to make sure it is always up and functioning properly. If not, switch to a more reliable server.

CHAPTER 8

HOW TO SPEND NOTHING ON STOCK

One of the most exciting bits about a trip to Ikea, the Swedish furniture store – apart from the joyful realisation that you've managed to survive the experience relatively unscathed and can go home – is the moment when you visit the Market Hall warehouse area downstairs to collect the smaller items you need yourself, having already written down the row letter and shelf number from the display upstairs. The shelves reach to the ceiling and stretch far out into the distance, piled high with products, and the sheer scale of it takes your breath away. It is overwhelming, once you realise just how much stock there is, how much money has been needed to buy it and house it and transport it, and how much there needs to be available at any time for customers to buy, all piled up, multiplied by all the Ikea shops in the world.

If you are starting a business without any money, it is obviously going to be a lot easier starting a service-based venture than a product-based one because a service-based business doesn't require you to hold any stock. You provide the service – whether that is plumbing, dressmaking or IT skills – and people pay you for it. Easy.

Even better, you can offer a service either in person or online. Abi Wright's venture, Spabreaks.com, for example, is an online booking service for people wishing to book treatment packages and short breaks at spas in large hotels, which typically consist of a pool, sauna, steam room, whirlpool bath and treatment room. Customers can book their spa breaks via the website or by phoning her call centre – either way, Abi doesn't actually provide the spa breaks herself, she simply advises customers on the most suitable hotel for their needs and then takes a commission from the hotel for every booking made. She launched the site in 2008 with twenty-six venues offering day or overnight-stay spa packages and her firm, which now also offers spa holidays, has a turnover of £11 million a year.

Abi says: 'My plan had always been to keep it simple. I didn't want to cause problems for the hotels by wanting exclusive this or that – we just sold what they were selling, but through a different medium.'

Products can work, too

The good news, though, is that starting a business which sells products is entirely possible too without money, provided you think a bit creatively.

Let's take a look. The need to hold large stocks of products is a big problem for any start-up because that requires a lot of money not only to buy the products, but also to store them, to transport them, to distribute them and even to insure them. What's more, that money spent on stock stays tied up. It is no good Ikea selling everything in its warehouse and then surveying the empty shelves and wondering what happens next – it has to constantly and immediately replenish anything sold with new stock and maintain the overall stock levels so it always has enough for its customers' requirements.

Happily there are several ways of not having to do any of the above and still create a thriving product business.

It's particularly easy to deal with the stock issue if you are starting an online web-based operation. What's the difference between a high street shop full of products to buy and a website full of pictures of products to buy? The answer is that while the high street shop actually has to have the products sitting there on the shelves, the web-based business only needs to have pictures of them – and to be able to get its hands on the products customers order quickly enough to enable them to send them out straight away. Provided it has a good ordering and delivery system backing it up, the internet venture doesn't actually need to hold any products at all.

And that small but powerful shift is the reason why you can start a product-based business without any money.

There are two main ways of doing this:

▶▶   You can create a website – known as a portal – which acts as a marketplace for selling other people's products. That way you don't actually need to hold any stock yourself; you simply direct the sales you get to the product providers and charge them a commission on every sale via your website.

▶▶   You can adopt a just-in-time approach, in which you sell the products directly yourself, but only order them from suppliers as and when an order comes in. As the business grows you can gradually build up your own stocks of the more popular items, using money generated from previous sales, while continuing to order the less popular items as you need them.

It pays to specialise

Whichever method you adopt, the best way to get your online marketplace noticed is to specialise in a particular product category. A quick scan through the internet reveals websites solely devoted to selling all kinds of single-product categories – hats (hatsandcaps.co.uk), cheese (justcheese. co.uk), liquorice (liquoriceworld.com) and even walking sticks (walkingsticksonline.co.uk).

The global reach of the internet means that specialising in almost any kind of niche has become possible in a way that it would never have been in the real, offline world. That's because whatever niche it is, thanks to the wide reach of the internet there are likely to be enough potential customers out there to make the numbers work.

When done well, customers like buying from specialist online marketplaces because they make life easier by providing everything related to a particular product in one place.

As the owners of Walkingsticksonline.co.uk say on their website, 'Specialist retailers are hard to find on the high street, but the internet is a different story altogether. We like to be able to confidently say yes to all enquiries.'

The best of these types of website also provide useful relevant information, too – the walking sticks website gives advice on how to choose a walking stick, for example, as well as the length you need and the difference between handle types. The cheese website has a recipe section (although more than one recipe would be useful).

Some of these specialist websites work by directing orders through to the sellers; others work by pre-buying in small quantities of the stock they sell; others simply order what they need from their suppliers when orders are placed with them. The wonderful thing is, provided it is done seamlessly and well, it is impossible to tell which model is used by which website. Provided the goods arrive as advertised, on time, in perfect condition, the customer need never know – and will certainly not care – which it is.

Even Amazon has got in on the act of selling things on behalf of other people. Having started in a fairly conventional way by selling books direct from its warehouse, it has now turned itself into the ultimate online marketplace by selling anything and everything on behalf of other businesses. Customers can order garden furniture, or toys, or even shoes, via the Amazon website. But it doesn't actually stock any of these things itself, it simply acts as the middleman and sends your order through to the garden furniture or toymaker which does, which will then deal with your order and send your goods direct to you itself.

The just-in-time approach

If you had taken a look at Ryan Kliszat's online shoe shop, Saysshoes.co.uk, when he had just launched it, you would have thought he had an enormous warehouse somewhere, stacked high with merchandise. He didn't. Initially Ryan had just a single pair of each of the popular sizes of the shoe styles he sold, with the shoes ready to be replenished within hours from the distributor when a sale was made.

The just-in-time approach not only enabled Ryan to launch his business on a minimal budget, it also saved him a fortune in stock and storage costs. It reduced, too, the possibility of him ever being left with a glut of unwanted product.

He says: 'Doing it this way gave me so much more scope. Just because you don't want to invest huge amounts of capital in stock doesn't mean you can't think like a big retailer.'

As the venture has grown Ryan has been able to use the money it generates to buy more stock and has now built up enough stock to be able to fulfil instantly the orders he receives himself. But as a way of starting out without much money, it was invaluable.

In order for this kind of system to work you need to have absolute faith that your suppliers are actually going to deliver the products you need when you need them to, and are not going to let you down. You also need to have a really efficient communication system between you and your supplier. Emails which are checked regularly by both sides is the most basic essential. But, preferably, you want to be able to have such a good relationship with your suppliers that they will give you access to information – ideally real-time online information – about how much stock they hold, so you can see what is available and so can be confident about taking orders, knowing the stock will be ready to be delivered when you need it.

As Ryan says: 'The holy grail is to be able to access the supplier's stock system. The secret is to be able to automate your re-ordering so you don't have to ring the suppliers up each time and wait for someone to ring you back and take your order. Some suppliers are more forward-thinking than others.'

Andy Reedman is the founder of Mywarehouse.me, a pay-as-you-go order fulfilment firm which packs and posts orders on behalf of lots of start-ups and small businesses. Andy says the just-in-time model is becoming increasingly common among small online operations. Typically, small firms will monitor their stock levels every day, he says, then place an order with a distributor by 5 p.m. for delivery the next day.

Apart from the huge cost savings in not having to buy in lots of stock before you sell it, there are other advantages to adopting a just-in-time model. For a start, you can test out different products to see which ones sell without having to commit to them financially. All you need do is put up a picture of the product on your website that you wish to sell. If orders start to come in, then great, you can process them – if they don't, you can quietly take the picture down from the website and find something else to sell. All you will have wasted is the time spent uploading a photo and writing a few words to describe it.

A big factor in making possible this shift towards an ultra-lean approach has been a change in the attitude of whole-salers and distributors. In the past many of them adopted a rather snooty attitude towards small firms wishing to place small orders – or at the very least a 'can't be bothered' atti-tude. But now increasing competition and a greater awareness of small firms' potential has prompted a change of heart among many distributors. Not only are many now happy to take small orders, many offer free delivery for orders as little as £50.

Gareth Limpenny is typical of the new wave of distribu-tors who are supportive of small firms. As well as supplying all the major high street retailers, his firm Frequency Telecom also supplies mobile phone handsets and accessories to small firms across the country. It has set up a password-protected website so they can order their products online through his website for next-day delivery.

Gareth says the key to start-ups making the just-in-time model a success is for them to monitor closely their sales on a daily basis – and find a distributor who has the resources not to let them down. His firm, for example, which last year had a turnover of £21 million, holds enough stock at its warehouse in Chessington, Surrey, to be able to meet all kinds of last-minute requests from the retailers he supplies.

He says: 'As a supplier, part of our offer to retailers must be the flexibility to give them options and choices and to make it as easy as possible for them to run their business. If they decide to run a promotion next week, for example, they can, as we can send them the stock immediately rather than waiting six weeks for products to arrive from overseas. Part of our job is to help them be profitable too.'

The 'just-in-time, order it only when you have an order' model also means you can sell a far larger range of products than you would have been able to, so enabling you to offer a much wider choice to customers. And because you don't have to commit to stocking them in advance, it means it doesn't matter if you only sell a few of some items.

This retailing strategy – of selling a small number of lots of different items, usually in addition to selling a large number of a few more popular items – has become known as 'the long tail'. What is so exciting about it is that it turns conventional microeconomics on its head, and for the first time makes it possible for small enterprises to realise big profits from selling small volumes of hard-to-find items to many customers, instead of only selling large quantities of a small number of popular items – where they are likely to face more competition.

But do make sure you have proper supplier contracts in place so each side knows exactly what they are supposed to be doing. And don't take on too many suppliers because they will quickly become difficult to manage. You need more than one, so that a single supplier doesn't have the power to disrupt your business, either by being unable to supply products or by demanding more favourable terms. But more than ten will soon become unmanageable from an administrative point of view, particularly if you are doing everything yourself. The ideal number is four or five because that way you have the opportunity to give them more volume and so they will be more loyal to you, and yet you can still build a relationship with each of them.

Go made-to-order

If you want to sell your own products without spending any money on stock upfront, that is possible, too. Even better, this approach works for on-the-ground ventures as well as online ones.

The secret is to offer made-to-order products for which customers will be willing to pay upfront – and will be prepared to wait until they are made. That way you will have received the money upfront which you can then spend on the raw materials you need to make the product.

Many businesses sell things with the promise of speedy delivery these days – Amazon offers a paid-for premium service called AmazonPrime which guarantees one-day delivery – but the truth is people are still usually prepared to wait for something which is nice and special and can't be bought anywhere else. The secret is to choose that kind of a product – and to have the skills to make it. Creative products such as wedding cakes, furniture, art, clothes and jewellery fit the model well, as do products requiring skilled knowledge, such as creating computer software. Even authors get paid upfront, in the form of an advance, long before they are required to deliver the product, their book.

The last time I bought a sofa I was astonished to discover I would have to wait twelve weeks for it to be delivered. Twelve weeks! I could probably have made a sofa myself in that time. But I still went ahead and bought it, and paid my money upfront and sat on the floor to watch television until it arrived, because I really liked that sofa and knew it would look lovely in my home. And because I couldn't find any other sofas I wanted instead for the same kind of price. If you can create a product which people are prepared to wait for, you are on to a winner.

How to get your hands on products to sell

Once upon a time suppliers were often happy to extend credit to new businesses; in other words supply them with the product they needed to buy and then invoice them for payment thirty days later. That meant if you were smart and on the ball you would be able to generate enough cash from selling your products to be able to pay the invoice when it became due, without having to borrow money from anyone. A lot of fledgling start-ups were able to get off the ground this way without any funding simply by adopting this method and trading on credit for a while.

Sadly, this isn't really possible any more, unless you know the supplier personally, because tighter credit controls and the possibility of bad debts means a new start-up with no previous trading history is unlikely to pass the credit check needed to get credit, at least until they have been trading a while.

The good news is there are still ways of finding products to sell that you don't have to pay upfront for – or, indeed, at all. All you need to do is to take something which nobody wants and sell it on to someone who does want it. It's a tried and tested formula, that someone's rubbish is someone else's treasure – after all, that's what lies behind the success of car boot sales, behind the idea of house clearance firms and behind television programmes such as *Cash in the Attic* and even *Antiques Roadshow*.

Tracey Banks has discovered how well this idea can work. She runs Enhance Image Consultancy, based in Longframlington, Northumberland, which advises clients about what type of clothes and styles suit them. Every few weeks she holds a one-day pop-up sale in a local coffee shop or village hall to sell all her clients' unwanted clothes on a profit-share basis. If the clothes sell she then splits the proceeds and gives half the money back to the client. If they don't, she simply gives them back.

The arrangement works a treat – it means Tracey has lots of good-quality clothes to sell, yet does not have to pay anything upfront for them, paying her clients – i.e. her suppliers – only if they are sold. And the clients whose clothes are sold are delighted because they are getting money for clothes which would otherwise have stayed stuffed at the back of their wardrobes taking up space. They don't even have to take them to Tracey themselves: she will pick the clothes up from their house.

She says: 'My house is currently bursting at the seams

with clothes. I am providing a service which is a bit different and people like that. The feedback I get is terrific.'

This method can work well for other products, too – if you are good with your hands you could offer to take people's broken toys or furniture off their hands, for example, which you can then fix and sell on.

ACTION PLAN

▶▶ **Think hard about whether a product or a service business would be right for you. Both offer their own challenges when starting without money; you just have to decide which challenge you would prefer.**

▶▶ **Now think about your own interests. Is there an area which you know something about and would love to specialise in? If so, start checking out the competition. Do specialist shops or online stores for it already exist? If not, why not? And if they do, look closely at how they operate and whether you could do it better.**

▶▶ **Attend an industry trade fair and chat to potential suppliers about how the market works. Are there lots of small suppliers or a handful of large ones? Collectively they will be able to provide a lot of free useful insight into what business model is likely to work.**

CHAPTER 9

HOW TO PRICE YOUR PRODUCT OR SERVICE

After doing some research into the market I've decided to price my mugs at £10 each. My mugs aren't competing with general all-purpose mugs bought purely for drinking out of – after all, if someone wants some of those, Argos sells a set of six plain white mugs for £3.99, i.e. 66.5p each. Instead, I'm really competing with the makers of other mugs which are given as gifts – and I've discovered that those kinds of mugs can cost a lot more than £10. Indeed, individual handcrafted mugs sell for up to £40 each. My mugs are not at that level, but I feel that people will be happy to pay £10 for a mug which says ENTREPRENEUR, because they are rather special and rather nice – and because there is no one else out there selling anything similar.

Ten pounds works from a cost point of view, too, because

it will give me a healthy profit margin even when I order small quantities. Also £10 is a nice round number so it is ideal for when I am selling mugs at conferences because I don't need to bother with change.

There is another reason as well. It means that when I need to start charging VAT on my mugs there will still be enough margin to incorporate that too. All businesses need to charge VAT on their sales – the current rate is 20 per cent, with the odd exception – once their turnover exceeds £77,000 in any 12 month period. As you may not be able to simply raise your prices to accommodate this at the time, then you need to make sure from the start that you have enough profit margin to be able to take the hit.

The price is right

Deciding on a price for your product can be a real headache when you are starting out, because it is so important to get right and yet so easy to get wrong. It is particularly vital to be thinking along the right lines when you are starting up without any money, because you simply cannot afford to make any expensive mistakes. You need sales to begin flowing in from day one.

Fortunately there are several free or low-cost ways to help you pitch it at the right level. When Christopher Ward was trying to choose a price for his eponymous watches, he came up with an unusual solution. He placed three advertisements for identical watches in newspapers over one weekend: one offering them for £99, another selling them for £179 and a third pricing them at £849. The £179 watch sold best, so he set the price at £179 and refunded the four buyers who had been happy to buy the watch at £849. His Christopher Ward watch company – which has the advertising slogan 'the cheapest most expensive watches in the world' – now has a turnover of £4.5 million a year and employs nine people.

If you are planning to sell direct to your customers, the simplest way to decide on the price of your product or service is to ask them how much they would be prepared to pay. You don't have to pay an expensive consultancy to do this for you – you can assemble your own focus group by inviting some friends and acquaintances round for an evening and asking them what they think. Give them a range – say £10, £12.50 and £15 – to pinpoint their responses. You can also get some useful responses by standing in the street and asking passers-by for their thoughts. Choose a time and place where people are strolling along in the afternoon sun rather than rushing past in their lunch break.

This process will also enable you to gauge whether it is simply the price which would stop people buying your product, or whether it is something more fundamental.

In general there are five things which will enable you to charge more than the competition for your products or services:

▶▶ Convenience – if your product is right in front of me and so is saving me the time and effort of heading across town in the rain, I will probably buy yours even though it is a bit more expensive.

This is how city-centre express versions of super-market chains are able to charge more for the same products than their big out-of-town versions

▶▶ Solving a problem which rival products don't – or at least doing it in a more elegant or efficient way

▶▶ Being better made, or more durable

▶▶ Having a technological edge

▶▶ Being new and different, or being regarded as being fashionable or cool

Sometimes you are going to need to make some early adjustments. When Tony Culpin started his business Moving Moments, which makes DVD recordings of older people talking about their lives for relatives to keep for posterity, he could not find any competitors to compare his venture with – one of the reasons he started it in the first place. So he priced his service at £500, based partly on the amount of time it took to make each DVD and partly on the feeling that, if families shared the cost, it would not be too onerous. Initially, he got several orders but, two years later, demand slowed, so he cut the price to £395.

Tony, who started the venture in Warrington, Cheshire, with two friends after being made redundant from his job in IT, says: 'The pricing is difficult. You have to make sure you don't under-price so it ends up costing you money and, if you charge too little, people think it is going to be rubbish. But you also don't want to price it out of the market. We thought £500 was what the market would stand, but a few people said it seemed a bit expensive. People loved the idea of it, but said they couldn't afford it.'

Value your product

Once you have set your price, don't be too quick to offer discounts unless there is a very good reason to. I received an email from Robert McCann, who had started up a business selling time capsules – reinforced non-degradable containers which can be filled with mementos and buried for future generations to find. His customers were mainly schools, construction firms and housing trusts and he was doing well, but he faced a dilemma – how much of a discount should he give for bulk orders, in particular a bulk order of sixty from a customer who also wanted some bespoke work done on their capsules?

He wrote: 'I can manage the production side of it, but where I am stuck is in what to allow as a discount. The buyer is anticipating a reduction for volume, and for me to pass on any savings in my transport costs. I am actually happy to do this as such an order would give me a really good foundation for the future, but at the same time I don't want to belittle my efforts. What would you consider would be an appropriate level of discount acceptable to both sides?'

I suggested that instead of considering accepting a discount for this order of his time capsules, Robert should actually be charging a premium because he was creating a bespoke product specifically for the customer, which had involved extra effort on his part. However, if Robert still wanted to offer a discount in order to foster good future customer relations then he should offer a small token gesture of, say, 5 per cent. But a better alternative would be to offer a discount in a non-monetary way, for example by offering free delivery for the order. That way he would be able to offer a sweetener while preserving the actual price of the product. Important because otherwise if word gets around then every customer will expect a 5 per cent discount – and the price is eroded.

Robert took my advice and stuck to his guns. His firm, Time Capsules, now gets big orders without needing to discount, charges more for bespoke wrappers, and is doing brilliantly.

Remember:

▸▸ Cherish the word 'bespoke' and treat it with the utmost respect – it is your password to making your product stand out from the crowd. Bespoke work should always command a premium price

▸▸ Beware of falling into the classic start-up trap of being overly grateful for 'big' orders at the expense of margins. While an order of sixty units might seem a lot when you are starting out, the customer doesn't need to know that – and it certainly won't seem like a lot when you are selling 10,000 a month

Hit the high street

If you are thinking of selling your products via a high street retailer or supermarket, there is a brilliant – and completely free – way of finding out what you should be charging: simply go and ask them what they think. Provided they are running a successful venture themselves, they will know everything about the market they operate in, so will know exactly what price they could sell your product at, and how it compares to the competition. They will probably even tell you how many you can expect to sell in a given period. Then you can work backwards and work out at what price you will have to sell your products to the retailer – typically 50 per cent of the retail price – and therefore whether you will still be able to make a profit on these numbers. And therefore whether it is actually worth your while selling your product in this way.

This is exactly what Mark Dickinson and Nick Robins did. When they decided to start a business selling brightly coloured, eye-catching cycle and ski helmets, they were confident their customers would pay more for them than for helmets already on the market. So on their website they initially priced their ski helmets at £89.99, a £20 premium to the price charged by competitors, and their road cycle helmets at £59.99, £10 more than the competition.

After talking to several high street retailers, however, and taking their helmets in to show them, the pair realised they had got it wrong. The market was dominated by big-name, established branded products, which in customers' eyes were tried and tested. As an unknown brand, pricing their helmets at a premium to their rivals would seriously limit their sales, particularly as their helmets did not offer any significant technological advantage, only a design difference.

So they cut the price of their ski helmets by £20 to £69.99, their road cycle helmets from £59.99 to £49.99. As a result their cycle helmets are now stocked by high street retailers Halfords and Evans Cycles, their ski helmets are on sale in Cotswold Outdoor shops, and their venture, Hardnutz, is thriving.

Mark says: 'We were a bit naive and possibly even a bit arrogant to think we could command some sort of premium as an unknown brand launching into a fiercely competitive market. We are still going to have a point of difference, because our helmets are vibrantly designed, and retailers are much happier with the price now.'

Even the biggest retail stores will be happy to offer their advice free if you have a product which could be of interest to them.

When Daniel Woolman first asked Asda if they would be interested in his invention, a clip-on deodorising spray which keeps wheelie bins fresh, he didn't even have a finished product to show them. He only had a single prototype of his product, Binifresh, which had cost him £1,000 to make.

'The prototype was like gold dust,' says Daniel, 'Whenever anyone asked if they could keep it, I would say no.'

Despite only having a prototype to look at, the buyer at Asda decided Daniel's spray would sell well at a retail price of £14.99 – and promptly ordered more than 5,000 of them. Meetings with John Lewis, Lakeland and Tesco were also fruitful and they, too, agreed to stock Binifresh. Daniel has since launched the Minibini, a clip-on spray for kitchen bins, and his business is doing really well.

John Lewis is also happy to advise on every aspect of a product from price to quality. 'We like to work with small companies and make a success story of them,' says Elaine Whiteman, the toys and books buyer for John Lewis, which has twenty-nine stores. 'Their idea could be the next big thing and we want to be involved in that from the beginning.'

Elaine works with several small toy suppliers and there is always the potential to take on more small suppliers as 50 per cent of the toys stocked in John Lewis each season are new products. The best way to get in touch with the John Lewis buying team is via their website, Johnlewispartnership.co.uk. Even if they decide not to take on a product, they will offer feedback on both it and the packaging.

Michael Hall had been selling his children's horse-shaped swings made from recycled tyres through garden centres when he contacted the buyers at John Lewis. Within three months, he had received an order for the swings, which retail at £79.95. Since then, John Lewis has asked Michael to make a dinosaur swing and he is also working on a wooden version. Now John Lewis accounts for most of his firm's production.

Apart from the many forms which need to be filled in, supplying a large retailer has been very straightforward, says Michael, who runs his business from Ludlow, Shropshire. 'The fact that we get the orders so far in advance has been fantastic for us. We look after them and they look after us.'

Argos is also interested in hearing from small firms – small firms supply about 20 per cent of the retailer's toys and nursery products. It occasionally holds open days for inventors and small suppliers to meet the buying team, an invaluable way to get feedback not just on pricing but on all other aspects of your product.

Remember that the price you can get for a product is likely to differ markedly depending on the type of environment you are selling it in. You will be able to get a much higher selling price for your product in an upmarket boutique, for example, than you would selling it on a market stall. However, that is only half the story. You are not only interested in what the final selling price is; you are interested in how much of it will find its way back to you. Your scarves might sell for £20 in a boutique, for example, and only £12 on a market stall, but if you are only getting half of that £20, in other words £10 for every scarf sold in the boutique, while you get to keep all of the £12 you sell your scarves for on the market stall, then you will be better off selling them on the market stall.

But the price you get is still not the whole story – you also need to take into account how many scarves you sell. If you sell ten a week in the boutique but only five a week on the market stall, you will be making £100 in sales from the boutique but only £60 in sales from the market stall. What's more, selling them in the boutique might raise the profile of your scarves and of your business in general, to the extent that they are spotted by an upmarket department store which decides they would like to stock them, too. Who said business was complicated . . .

Selling to the big boys and girls

At some stage in this process you will need to decide if you actually want to start selling your products through a supermarket or big high street retailer. To some extent the decision will be made for you; if the retailer does not want to stock your product, or if you are not able to supply it at the price they are prepared to sell it at, then that spells the end of the matter.

But if they like your product and would like to take the discussion further, you need to think carefully about three things:

▶▶ Are you keen to build a brand of your own, or are you happy to create a business where you sell unbranded products – known as 'white label' products – to a retailer which will sell them under their own brand? Under a 'white label' arrangement, a firm supplies their products to a supermarket or high street retailer which then brands them with their own name, or label, for example Tesco's Finest range, or Sainsbury's Taste the Difference range. The selling price – and hence the profit margins – are typically less than you would achieve by selling the products under your own brand, but you are likely to be able to sell a greater volume.

Either option may be possible, but unless you product is really special the retailers are likely to

prefer a 'white label' deal – because your
products will boost their own brand range – so you
need to be clear in your own mind about what you
want before you enter into a discussion

▶▶ The price – be prepared for a shock. Selling through
a retailer of any kind is going to be a painful experience compared to selling direct to customers via
your website, because you have to factor in their
profit margins, too. If you sell via your website you
will get 100 per cent of the retail price; if you sell
via a retailer you will get half that. If you are not
able to make a profit at this level then you will
need to rethink

▶▶ If you decide to sell your products through a
retailer you will need to come to an agreement
with them about whether you can still sell via your
website. Some larger retailers may insist on exclu-
sivity and refuse to let you do this, on the grounds
that it is competition for their firm. Others will be
happy to let you continue selling via your website
provided the product is offered at the same, or a
higher, price

Before approaching any high street retailer with your product
or prototype, make sure you have done your research. Go
into their stores and have a look at their existing range of
products and think about where yours might fit in, both in
terms of price and quality. Then think about how yours

might offer something a bit special or different from what they already sell.

If you do decide you want to sell via a high street retailer or supermarket, the good news is that you have chosen a good moment to go about it. There was a time when the retailers were not interested in Britain's small businesses because they could not supply on the mass scale needed to fill the shelves of the national chains. Not any more. In the past few years there has been a big shift among large retailers towards buying from small enterprises, in the belief that entrepreneurs bring innovation and freshness to their shelves.

This is particularly true if you are a small food producer selling local or regional products. The big supermarkets are keen to expand their range of local products because customers love them – and also because they can often charge a premium for them. In Ocado, the online super-market, speciality artisan bread maker Gail's malted brown bloomer sells for £3.99 a loaf for example, compared to just £1.20 for Ocado's own-brand white bloomer of the same size.

Tesco holds regional roadshows for small food producers, where they can meet the supermarket's senior buyers face to face. Sainsbury's has a programme called Supply Something New, to make it easier for small suppliers by providing free training days, technical support and supplier certification. Waitrose's Locally and Regionally Produced Initiative now includes almost 1,200 product lines.

How to do it right

▶▶ Make your product as regionally identifiable as possible. Provenance is the buzz word right now – customers love knowing where the ingredients come from.

▶▶ Don't worry about how small you are – small producers with Tesco and Waitrose supply their products to between only ten and twenty stores on average, and both supermarkets have taken on small producers who make only enough to supply one store.

▶▶ Work out your cost price – in other words the minimum price at which you would be prepared to sell to the supermarket. This is the cost of making your product, plus the cost of packaging and delivery, plus a profit for yourself. There is no hard and fast rule about how much profit you should be making on each item sold, but you need to be comfortable that it reflects the effort and risk involved.

▶▶ Think about how you are going to deliver your products to the supermarket – and how you can make it cost-effective. Few supermarkets accept direct deliveries to a store, so you will have to take your goods to a central distribution depot which might be fifty miles away. One solution is to join forces with another producer in your area to share costs.

▶▶ If your product is taken on by a supermarket, get involved in promoting it. Make sure it is being displayed properly and offer to do in store tastings.

ACTION PLAN

▶▶ **Research your market thoroughly to find out where your product or service fits in.**

▶▶ **If in doubt, price high and adjust later.**

▶▶ **If you feel you need to offer a discount for bulk orders, reduce the total cost to the customer in other ways, for example by offering free delivery rather than lowering the unit price.**

CHAPTER 10

GET THE CASH FLOW RIGHT

Cash flow may sound like the most boring subject in the world. But it is the number one thing to get right if you are starting an enterprise without any money. Indeed, a staggering 90 per cent of small business failures are due to poor cash flow, according to Dun & Bradstreet, the business information company. You could have a fantastic product or service, wonderful customers and a brilliant business plan, but if you don't get your cash flow right then your firm will go bust. It is that scary, and it is that simple.

At its most basic, cash flow is a measure of the amount and timing of cash coming into and being paid out of your business each week. It is a snapshot of your actual cash position at any given time. If you have no money in your bank account and you need to pay your supplier £200 on Wednesday, then it is going to make a big difference to both you and him whether the £300 you are owed from a customer is paid to you the day before, on the Tuesday, or the day after, on the Thursday. A firm with good cash flow will create a pattern of income and spending which allows it to always have enough cash available to pay bills on time.

Cash flow should not be confused with revenue, or income, which is simply the amount of money which has been promised to you but which may or may not have actually shown up yet. It is the difference between holding a piece of paper with a number written on it, and holding banknotes and coins in your hand. You may have sold a lot of products in a week, but unless you have actually received the money for them it is not going to hold much sway with the man on the doorstep who needs to be paid for the raw materials or equipment he is delivering, and nor is it going to pay that outstanding electricity bill. When you get paid for an order is just as important as taking the order in the first place.

Kate Castle is busy learning the art of managing cash flow at her business, Boginabag. She had the idea for Boginabag in 2008 while camping in Dorset. Lying awake and needing to go to the loo, she decided there must be a better option than having to trek across a dark campsite to a toilet block. On her return home, she started hunting around for a portable toilet which she could take with her next time. But all she could find were bulky chemical-based toilets, so she decided to create a better alternative herself. Two years later, having navigated patents, product design and prototypes, her portable toilet, Boginabag, was born. It is a lightweight, folding three-legged stool with a hole in the seat, and it comes with a pack of five absorbent disposable bags. They fit over the hole and can be tied at the top and thrown away after use.

So far so good; that was the easy bit. The hard bit has been managing the cash flow of her business because her Boginabags are manufactured in China and shipped over to be sold via her website. When she places an order with the factory in China, Kate has to pay 30 per cent of the total cost upfront and the remaining 70 per cent while the goods are being transported to her. It takes at least thirty days for the toilets to be made, and then another thirty days to be shipped to the UK. But she doesn't get any money in from customers until she actually sells them, weeks or even months later.

Sales of her Boginabag soared after Kate appeared on the BBC television programme *Dragons' Den* demonstrating how it would be ideal for campers and festival-goers. It immediately captured the imagination of viewers and as a result sales are expected to leap from £28,000 in 2011 to £150,000 in 2012.

Great news for Kate's profit figures – but ironically that simply made the cash flow situation even worse, as she suddenly needed to spend far more on buying in new stock than she had so far received from customers for toilets already sold – and pay the money out at least two months before seeing any of it back.

'When I started I don't think I realised how important cash flow is,' says Kate, who works from home in Winchester. 'But it is a big issue for me.'

Fortunately for Kate, as well as boosting sales, her appearance on *Dragons' Den* also led to one of the dragons, Theo Paphitis, investing £50,000 in return for a 30 per cent stake, giving her much-needed working capital which she can use to fund the purchase of new stock.

Sadly that kind of publicity and celebrity assistance is not something that you can count on happening to you and your fledgling start-up. So you need to make sure your cash flow works in your favour right from the start. Getting the cash flow structure right is particularly vital when you are starting up a business without any cash, because you don't have the security of a buffer of cash in the bank account to dip into if your incomings and outgoings don't quite match up.

The secret is to match your cash flows. In other words to get money in from customers before – or at least at the same time as – you have to pay it out to suppliers. That way you always have a positive cash balance and you always know the money is sitting in your account waiting for you to use.

There are seven main ways to ensure you get the cash in before you have to pay it out:

1. Get paid upfront

Getting paid for your product or service before you actually have to give it to the customer is the single best way to start a business without cash, and I am constantly amazed at how few small firms try to do it.

It's easy if you are selling to individual customers, of course. As customers we automatically expect to have to pay upfront for the products or services we buy, even if we have to wait ages to actually take delivery – and the internet has made this even more prevalent. We think nothing of giving our debit or credit card details for everything from food delivery to clothes, to hotel rooms and holidays. I recently bought some old-style video tapes via the internet for my old-style video camera, paying upfront for them with my debit card, and they took so long to arrive that by the time they did I had completely forgotten I had ever ordered them.

The great thing about being paid upfront is that if you have chosen the right product or service to sell, you too can get the money in from your customers before you have to pay it out to your suppliers. This is the principle on which events organisers operate, for example, and it means you don't actually need to borrow any money because you are always cash flow positive.

If you are selling to other businesses, things become a little more complicated. Businesses typically like and expect to be able to pay thirty days in arrears, with you sending them an invoice after you have supplied the goods or services. That makes it more of a challenge when starting up a venture without any money. But it doesn't have to be that way, and the advent of direct debit and the ability to take payment online and over the phone has made it much easier for small firms to take payment immediately.

If you are selling to a business customer who does not like the idea of paying upfront, then give them a real financial incentive to do so by offering them a discount off the price, or by giving them a (useful) additional service. And, if you can, sign them up to direct debit, which takes the money owed automatically from their bank account. In fact, make direct debit your new best friend. If you can get customers to pay directly into your bank account then you will save yourself enormous amounts of time and bother dealing with paperwork and chasing up late payments. And not only does it ensure you get paid promptly; if there is a recurring charge, for example a monthly or annual renewal fee to pay, it ensures you will get that on time, too, without even having to ask for it.

You may protest that some industries don't work that way, and it is hard for a newcomer to change the rules. But if you don't ask, you won't get – and you will never know if you could have got. Simple as that.

If you are a tradesperson, for example, make it clear in advance that customers must pay on the spot for work done. I recently had my boiler fixed (again . . .) and when the plumber came to fix it I got my cheque book out to pay him there and then. But he simply tore off an invoice from his pad, filled it in and said I could pay later if I wanted. I inevitably mislaid the invoice and forgot all about it and only ended up paying it several months later, after the firm had called me and sent me a new invoice. I got it and paid it – but what if I had moved house in the meantime? They might never have been able to track me down and would have had to write off the debt. What a pointless waste of time and effort. And if all their customers are doing the same thing, what a crazy way to run a business.

2. Match your cash flows

Getting your customers to pay upfront or soon after is only one half of the cash flow story, however. You also need to make sure that whatever is happening with your customers is mirrored by what is happening with your suppliers.

If you can't persuade your business customers to pay upfront for your products or services then you at least need to try and get the flows of cash working in your favour and get payment in before you have to pay it out. If you need to pay your suppliers thirty days after receiving their goods and services – known as thirty-day payment terms – for example, then try to persuade your customers to pay you quicker than that, for example fourteen days after they receive their goods and services from you.

3. Buy small

Choose a product which you can buy in small quantities so you are not tying up a lot of money in stock each time. Yes, it will probably cost a bit more per unit – suppliers generally give discounts for larger quantities so initially your unit cost will be higher – but it will also mean you can keep your money requirements really small. The secret to making this work is to find a product or service which can command a high margin, in other words a big difference between cost price and selling price, so that it can accommodate your higher initial cost price. In this case, even though the margins will be smaller than they would if you were buying larger quantities, you will still make a profit on each sale. You will not be able to use this model if the margins are too low because initially you will be selling at a loss, which is a certain route to disaster. Buying in at £4, selling at £6 – good; buying in at £3, selling at £6 – better; buying in at £7, selling at £6 – bad.

4. Make friends with your supplier

If your business model is based on the idea that you will order what you need from your suppliers after you have taken an order from a customer, then you need to make sure you have very strong supplier agreements in place – ideally backed up by a relationship with one person in the supplier firm who you can get to know personally and talk to as often as you need. There is nothing worse than customers wanting to buy a product from you and you not actually being able to get it for them. Not only will you wreck that particular sale, you will also seriously tarnish the reputation of your business if customers think you cannot be trusted to fulfil their order properly – and they will also tell their friends.

5. Ensure customers are creditworthy

You also need to check that your customers are in a position to be able to pay you in the first place. To do this you need to run a credit check on them before you agree to trade with them. A credit check will look at their financial position and see whether they have failed to pay others in the past, among other things. Some high street banks now offer a limited free credit checking service for their customers, for example for up to five businesses – ask yours what they can offer you. You can also ask a credit checking agency such as Experian or Equifax for a credit check report. Findout (findoutinfo.com), the business credit checking arm of Equifax, for example, charges a few pounds for a Business Essentials Report, which includes trade references and information on any county court judgements against a company.

You can also do some credit checking yourself, which has the advantage that it is free – ask the customer for a copy of its latest filed accounts and up-to-date management accounts. Also ask for trade references which you can call to check if the customer pays on time and is straightforward to deal with. You could also speak to the trade association which represents your customer's industry. Sometimes it may be willing to tell you if a company is bad news.

A word of warning, too: beware new clients who suddenly give you a big order – it may be that they have been refused credit by their regular suppliers. So ask around your industry contacts to find out the real story, and if in doubt refuse to take the order unless they agree to pay upfront.

6. Invoice properly

You need to get your invoicing procedure right. The best way to ensure you get paid promptly by a big firm is to send the invoice on time to the right person at the right place, and make sure it contains all the details which are needed to get it through their payment system. You may need to include a particular reference number, for example. If in doubt, ring them up and check. A large customer is going to have loads of invoices to process and if you don't get things right on your invoice it will be left to languish at the bottom of the pile.

You might also want to remind them in the small print on your invoice that all firms now have the right to charge late-payers interest on outstanding amounts, under the Late Payment of Commercial Debts (Interest) Act. Often simply reminding customers you can charge this will encourage them to pay up.

Finally, make sure you keep good records as to exactly when the money is coming in and out of your business account. Not only will this be really useful for you, it will be really useful to be able to show your bank manager, any potential investors, and, indeed, customers who in turn want to do some credit checking on you.

7. Chase all payments

There is no point in putting all this cash flow structure in place if you don't monitor and police it properly. If someone owes you money, chase it up until you get it. Contact the customer a few days before the bill is due to remind them it needs paying, and then ring them the day it is due, and then continue to ring them until it is paid. Small businesses are often squeamish about ringing people to ask them for money, especially if it is someone with whom they have a good working relationship. But you must protect your enterprise.

Anna Vivian has heard all kinds of excuses from late-paying clients. She runs Fastbadge Europe, a graphic design firm in Plymouth. Explanations from customers paying late have so far included: the person responsible for signing the cheques is on holiday; the accounts department has no direct phone line and can only be contacted by email; someone new has joined the company and, because she is unfamiliar with the systems, it's unclear which bills she has and hasn't paid.

She says: 'Some customers will do anything to lengthen the time it takes to pay. It does help to keep hassling them but it is all time out of your day and is very frustrating.'

Susan Hallam is the founder of Hallam Internet in Nottingham, a marketing services firm. To reduce late payments she has recently hired a book-keeper who comes in two days a month to chase unpaid invoices. 'She is my terrier on the telephone,' says Susan, 'I wish I had done it previously. It brings money into our account the day after she starts chasing them. She is worth every penny.'

With the help of an adviser, Susan has also created a spreadsheet giving her a weekly snapshot of the cash coming in and going out. She also credit-checks every potential client. She says: 'The biggest difference is I can now sleep at night. I know exactly where I stand.'

By being paid on time, you will not only ensure the survival of your business, you will also save yourself a fortune in unplanned borrowing such as unauthorised overdrafts and emergency credit card limit extensions which you would need to cover the cash flow gap left by the customer not paying their bills. Banks make an enormous amount of money in one-off fees from customers going over previously agreed limits. If you can avoid being one of them, so much the better.

ACTION PLAN

▶▶ Run a credit check on every new business customer and take up trade references.

▶▶ Chase invoices as soon as they become due and don't be fobbed off with excuses. Call every day until they are paid.

▶▶ Establish a good – ideally personal – relationship with all your suppliers.

CHAPTER 11

HOW TO SPEND NOTHING ON MARKETING

When Michelle Stephenson recalls her experiences as an exhibitor at a trade fair in Olympia to promote her fledgling enterprise Sapphire Education and Training, she is unsure whether to laugh or cry.

Having taken a stand at a technology in education fair in 2011 to promote a compendium of PowerPoint games for teachers to use as lesson starters, Michelle found herself tucked away in a tiny cubicle in a corridor, with just one friend to help her, having woefully underestimated how much the whole venture would cost. By the time the four-day event was over she had spent £5,000 on the exercise, including pop-up banners, marketing, accommodation and travel, but made sales of just £500.

Michelle, who started her business without any money,

running it in her spare time from her home in Cheshire while holding down a full-time job as a teacher, says: 'The stand was the size of a telephone cubicle. It cost about £1,800 and I didn't factor in the fact I would also have to pay for other things such as a table, a chair and a PA system, so the costs just kept going up and up. It was a very steep learning curve.'

At first glance, taking a stand at a trade show might seem like the ideal way for a small firm to get their products in front of a large number of potential customers at once. Trade fairs are big business these days. In 2010 nearly 1.8 million people attended 260 trade shows between them in the UK, covering every industrial sector from food processing to aerospace, according to data collected by Facetime, the marketing body for the events industry.

But while trade fairs can be beneficial for some firms, they can also be an expensive minefield for a first-time entrepreneur learning the ropes. As well as the cost of the stand itself – and getting yourself and your team to the event – you are likely to find yourself having to pay for a whole raft of additional services such as marketing, AV equipment hire, storage, electricity, public liability insurance and furniture hire. You might even have to pay for someone to bring deliveries from the main gate to your stand.

There are other costly incidentals, too. You will need to think about how you are going to record the contact details of people visiting your stand, for example. Writing them all down by hand is extremely time-consuming – and, worse, takes you away from talking to potential consumers – so you may need to hire a data pen to scan the bar code on

ID badges. An ingenious solution to the problem, undoubtedly, but it will cost you an extra £250 you weren't planning to spend.

All of which means that you need to think hard about whether the investment will really pay off.

In fact, trade fairs are just one way of tearing through your non-existent start-up budget – there are actually lots of ways in which you could theoretically spend a fortune. The biggest potential black hole for pouring your money into is the one marked 'marketing and promotion'. Indeed, some entrepreneurs are so hard-wired into thinking they need to spend a fortune on this, they don't even stop to consider whether they really do. I spoke to one bank manager who said she sometimes gets people coming in and airily saying they will need a marketing budget of £100,000 to promote their new business. Funnily enough, the answer is always no.

The good news is that all this talk of the need for vast marketing budgets is nonsense. There are hundreds of ways of promoting your product or service for little or no cost. All you have to do is be inventive, and fearless. Fearless not because you could lose money, but because people close to you might laugh at you for having outlandish ideas. But, hey, they probably laughed when you told them you wanted to start up a business; you ignored them then and so you can ignore them again now.

Stand out from the crowd

The simplest way of promoting your product is to make the product or service itself stand out in some way, so people cannot fail to notice it. David Seymour did this quite literally at his firm Everbuild Building Products, when on a whim he decided to colour the instant bonding adhesive he had created pink, rather than the usual grey or brown which other industrial adhesives came in. For good measure, he even called it Pinkgrip. Most people who worked for his business thought he was completely mad. After all, the product was being sold to, and used by, hard-bitten tradesmen engaged in heavy-duty building projects. Undaunted, David ordered 20,000 tubes – and it sold out within an hour of going on sale. Within three months Pinkgrip had become the company's best-selling product.

David says: 'I knew this product was really special, but if we had just called it "instant grab adhesive" then nobody would have noticed it. It got builders talking.' Thanks in part to the enormous success of Pinkgrip, David's business now has 230 employees and an annual turnover of £52 million.

Nick Grey got people talking about his product in an even more dramatic way. When he invented a cordless sweeper he showed it to a former colleague – who introduced him to an American firm which specialised in selling small appliances through television shopping channels. They agreed to sell Nick's sweepers this way too. Even better, the arrangement not only cost Nick absolutely nothing, it even generated an upfront payment – under the licensing deal, the American firm paid him US $60,000 (around £37,500) upfront and royalties on subsequent sales.

His sweeper was shown on the shopping channel under the name Shark Sweeper.

The impact was instant. Nick says: 'It just went ballistic. I remember getting a phone call saying the product was sold out everywhere. I started bouncing up and down the hall. For a while, it was the best-selling small appliance in America. The beauty of TV shopping is that when it hits, it really hits.'

At its peak, Grey was getting an income of £250,000 a month from his share of sales. The following year, using the money he had made he was able to launch the sweeper in Britain under his own brand, Gtech. It is now stocked in Argos, John Lewis and Currys and his firm has a turnover of £8 million with thirty staff.

Word of mouth

One effective – and free – way of promoting your venture is simply to get your customers to do it for you, by good old-fashioned word of mouth. If you can get people talking about your product in a positive way and telling others how fabulous it is, they will promote it far better than you, or, indeed, an expensive advert, could ever do.

When Angus Wielkopolski started selling goats' milk at his farm near Howden in north Humberside, he got his customers talking about it, and telling other people about it, simply by putting pictures of his customers on the side of the cartons. Now every carton of St Helen's Farm goats' milk carries a picture of one of their customers together with a story about the farm and the animals. The picture and the story which goes with it are changed every month and the idea has become so popular there is currently a six-month waiting list of people wishing to be featured.

Angus says: 'We have a lot of satisfied customers who love our products and they queue up to go on the milk cartons. They feel they are part of a club. They identify with us and the farm and they don't feel they are just getting an anonymous product from a factory.'

His inspired idea has clearly paid off. Having started out with just 300 goats bought for £40 each, his business, St Helen's Farm, now has 6,000 goats and is the biggest goats' milk processor in the UK, supplying all the major supermarkets. The operation also makes goats' cheese, goats' yoghurt and goats' butter, and has a turnover of £26 million and employs 100 people.

Word of mouth works brilliantly for service businesses, too. Lisa Shell has an enviable confession to make: she has never spent a penny on marketing her eponymous architectural practice, which is based in north London. That's because about 80 per cent of her work comes through word of mouth recommendations. Indeed, despite the current tough economic climate, her practice is in such demand she regularly turns away work.

Lisa, whose firm carries out private residential alterations and refurbishments and employs three people, says: 'I don't spend any time or money finding work – people ring me up instead of the other way round. We will often get a call from someone saying they have seen the work we did at a friend's house and would love to talk to us.'

As well as being an inexpensive way of getting work, there are other advantages to getting business this way.

Lisa says: 'The benefit is that our clients come to us feeling confident rather than feeling on edge, or that they have to test us, because they have seen what we have done and have heard how it went.'

Study after study shows customers respond far more favourably to personal recommendations from friends or colleagues than they do to paid-for advertising. So how do you go about harnessing it in the most effective way?

The first step is obviously to provide a product or service which people are actually going to want to talk about and encourage their friends to try. The last thing you want is for them to start telling their friends how rubbish it is.

The next step is to actively encourage customers to start spreading the news – both in person and online. It is no good simply sitting back and hoping it will happen. Give your customers cards which offer discounts for them to give to friends and family. Ask their permission to display their positive testimonials on your website or promotional flyers.

Send a postcard

Indeed, simply staying in touch can work wonders. I was surprised to receive a lovely New Year's greetings card from France this year, with a picture of a nice looking farmhouse on the front and a handwritten note inside wishing us well and inviting us to come and stay again. I didn't recognise the signature. It took me a while to work out that the card was actually from the owners of a *chambre d'hôtes* near Poitiers which we stayed in last year while visiting friends nearby. The card listed all the contact details and the nightly rates for the coming year, and if I had been planning a return visit it would have been much simpler – and therefore much more likely to happen – to call them than start scouring the internet in the hope that I might remember the name of the place where we had stayed.

Traditional word of mouth does have its limits, however, simply because it takes time to build up a reputation and even longer for word to get around. Which is where the internet comes in. Customers' opinions about a product or service can spread a million times faster in the online world than it ever could in the real world because of the extraordinary reach of the internet. Social networking sites such as Facebook, Twitter and YouTube mean what would once have taken months to percolate through the community now takes seconds. And it's a much bigger community.

Spreading the word about a product or service can work best when online social networking is combined with some real-life, real-people interaction, too. Maria Hatzistefanis has been generating a word of mouth buzz for her skincare products this way ever since she launched her beauty business, Rodial, several years ago.

Instead of waiting for customers to start talking about her products, she actively encourages people to get excited about them by sending samples of products to influential beauty industry bloggers to review up to six months before a new product is launched.

She also writes her own blog on the company's website and gives out advance information on Facebook and Twitter.

In addition, she has 100,000 registered customers who are kept informed about new products and sends products to some twenty unofficial brand ambassadors – customers who regularly use social media sites to share their views.

Maria, whose company sells skincare products with catchy names such as Tummy Tuck, Boob Job and Bum Lift, all of which offer an alternative to plastic surgery, says: 'In the past few years, social media have helped a lot with creating a word of mouth buzz. They work even better than advertising. We have occasionally invested in print advertising and the impact is nowhere near as great.'

She says word of mouth recommendations will typically double sales of a product. Her business, based in Fulham, south-west London, has annual sales of £5 million.

Of course, no matter what medium you use to deliver the message, people aren't going to pass the word on to their friends if your product or service hasn't made an impact on them or didn't stand out in some way. My fridge has been delivering everything you could ask of a fridge for years, and presumably has been giving me excellent value for money for years, and yet I have never felt the need to share this thrilling news with anyone. So the real challenge is to create a product or service which people are going to want to talk about and get excited about.

For Maria that means launching products with a story attached. One of her best-known products, for example, is called Snake Serum. It uses an ingredient which imitates the effect of snake venom in paralysing the muscles.

She says: 'If we were just selling scented body creams or a nice moisturiser, there would not be enough about the product to create a buzz. It is a combination of the right product with the right story that makes it interesting.'

The ultimate goal, of course, is for your customers to be so enthusiastic about spreading the word about your product or service that they become fans. That has happened at Apple, where customers often become so passionate about products such as the latest version of the iPad or iPhone that the queues round the block for the latest products become headline news.

Apple doesn't need to spend much on marketing its products because its customers are doing it all for them. They treat every product launch with the barely suppressed excitement usually only seen in four-year-olds waiting for their birthday.

Some of the ideas you try aren't going to work, of course. Fortunately if they have hardly cost you any money then it doesn't matter. I took out an advert to promote my entrepreneur mugs in *Private Eye*, the satirical magazine. It cost me £27.50 to run it in a single edition.

My advert read: 'Lovely mugs for entrepreneurs. The perfect gift. £10.'

My advert produced precisely zero responses. Still, it was a cheap way of finding out that this was definitely not going to be a reliable selling route for me.

One other thing – don't get so carried away by promotions which promise to bring in more sales that you forget to crunch the numbers and find out if it really is worthwhile doing. When Rachel Brown wanted to attract more customers to her cake-making venture, Need A Cake, she decided to run a promotion on her cupcakes through the discount website Groupon. However, even though she had been running her firm for twenty-five years, she made a classic mistake. She set the discounted price of her cupcakes far too low. She normally sold a box of twelve cupcakes for £26, but through Groupon Rachel rashly chose to offer a discount of 75 per cent, bringing the price of a box down to just £6.50.

When the promotion went up on the site, her business was promptly – and predictably – swamped with orders. Suddenly Rachel, who normally makes 100–150 boxes of cupcakes a month, found herself with orders for 4,500 boxes. As a result she had to take on more staff to cope and the whole thing started to spin out of control. She normally employs eight workers but had to bring in seventeen agency staff to help out in her firm, which is based in Woodley, near Reading. In total she had to spend an extra £12,500 on staff and distribution, which meant she was effectively making a loss of £2.50 on every box sold. In the end the promotion wiped out her profits for the entire year.

In general, voluntarily lowering the price of your product or service in order to promote it and draw attention to it is a bad idea. This is because:

▶▶   Yes, you may well attract lots of new customers – but they were mostly attracted by the discounted price and so will disappear as soon as you put it back up again. Therefore all that effort will achieve little in the long run. Few of Rachel Brown's new Groupon customers are likely to be returning to buy her cupcakes at £26 a box.

▶▶ By showing yourself to be willing to lower your prices whenever the mood takes you, you are sending out the message that the price can be tinkered with – and therefore people will come to expect discounts and will be reluctant to pay full price. And once you start having to discount your price merely to attract any kind of customers at all, you might as well give up and go home.

ACTION PLAN

▶▶ Help your customers to talk about you by giving them something to talk about – what makes your product or service stand out from the crowd?

▶▶ Use your packaging and website to tell the (true) story behind your product or service. It is a great free way of helping customers to remember you – and gives them something to tell others.

▶▶ Keep in touch with everyone who buys from you by postcard or email.

CHAPTER 12

HOW TO SPEND NOTHING ON PROMOTION

Promotion is one area where not having any money to spend can be a positive advantage. Even just a few years ago the opportunities for free promotion were fairly limited compared to the clout of paid-for advertising. Now, thanks to the proliferation of social networking and online media, paid-for advertising is in crisis and free is not only possible, it is expected. Which means that you really can make your lack of money go a very long way. Here's how.

Twitter

It took me a long time to warm to the idea of Twitter. The whole idea just really smacked of, we're all doing it, we're so cool, you're not, so you're not in our club. It reminded me of being at school and I instinctively wanted no part of it. People wittering away to their pretend friends about nothing. No thank you. But I eventually joined in 2010 because I was taking a one-woman show to the Edinburgh Fringe Festival that year; because my book, *How to Make a Million Before Lunch*, was about to be published; and mostly because everyone told me I should. I didn't get what it was for, though, especially because at the time most people seemed to be using it to tell other people what they had for breakfast. Even worse, there was this whole other language thing going on that you were supposed to somehow know, which I didn't – RT (retweet), DM (direct message) and #FF (follow Friday, in which you recommend other people to follow on Twitter). Horrible. Also, it felt completely counterintuitive – tweets which look as though they are addressed to one person can actually be read by anyone. No wonder so many people have tripped up and accidently told the world their private thoughts.

Also, I couldn't work out what to tweet. Once I had told everyone that a) I was taking a show to the Edinburgh Festival called 'How to Make a Million Before Lunch', and b) my book with the same title was being published at the same time, then what else was there of interest to say? I sent out the above messages several more times (apologies if you were one of my early followers, it must have been thrilling getting my tweets) then I gave up. Then I started telling everyone what I was writing about in the *Sunday Times* that week, then I started retweeting interesting things other people said, and when I launched my venture Entrepreneur Things,

Twitter was the first person I told. Several people even bought mugs as a result. But I still didn't really get it and was only on it because I thought I should be. I still secretly thought the whole thing was a massive waste of time.

But then something changed. Two things, actually. At round about tweet number 330, I got a tweet from Will King, the founder of King of Shaves, a successful entrepreneur and now a friend, who had seen one of my tweets about my mug business and suggested I get in touch with a wholesale distribution company he knew to talk to them about my mugs. Because he had mentioned the wholesaler's twitter handle, John, the owner of the firm, could see the message, see my twitter name (@rachelbridge100) and contact me directly, without ever having to bother Will. However, because Will was mentioned in the firm's tweet to me, he would be able to see a copy and know we had been in touch.

And then it clicked. The real magic of Twitter is being able to engage people in conversation and at the same time see what other people are saying about you. It's like eavesdropping on people talking about you, but with their consent. So then you have the option of responding, or getting involved, or not, as you see fit.

Anyway, John and I had a Twitter chat, and then a real-life chat, and we arranged that he would sell my mugs on Amazon and eBay for me, with no upfront cost or contract commitment, in return for a 70/30 split. In other words, he would take £3 of the £10 I sold each mug for and I would keep £7. A hefty slice of my profit, to be sure, leaving me with only a small margin per mug, but it was ideal. No money upfront, pay-as-you-go, and a great way to test the wider market without any effort on my part. And I figured that if we sold lots of mugs this way, the cost price of my mugs would fall anyway as I could order them in larger quantities from the supplier.

We agreed that I would initially send out the mugs from my own supplies (in my cellar), but if orders got large I could send a box of mugs to his warehouse and he would send them out from there.

John got on to it straight away and the next day he emailed me to say he had already sold five mugs, and here were the addresses for me to send them out to. Amazing. Would that ever have happened without Twitter? No.

The second thing that changed my mind about Twitter was a tweet I happened to see from a lady called Liz, who works for the Business and Education South Yorkshire Enterprise Exchange. She tweeted that she was looking for 'any product based biz willing to let a group from @PJEA_org Sheffield pitch their product to retailers in an apprentice style challenge'. After a quick bit of Googling I discovered that @PJEA_org was the Peter Jones Enterprise Academy, the learning institute set up by entrepreneur and *Dragons' Den* investor Peter Jones to help teach young people about entrepreneurship. So I replied, offering my mugs. Within hours Liz and I had spoken, I had discovered that the students would be pitching my mugs to the likes of John Lewis and Debenhams in Sheffield, I had arranged to speak to the students before they went to see the retailers, and I had put two mugs in the post to her. The most fantastic opportunity for me, to have people pitch my mugs to retailers on my behalf at absolutely no effort or cost to me, and something which I would never have found out about if it wasn't for Twitter. In the pre-Twitter days Liz would not even have been able to send a message out into the world like that.

The other point about Twitter is that you can instantly and directly contact the person you want in an organisation, no matter how high up they are or how unapproachable they normally are. Because at this stage of the game, if that person has made a point of going on Twitter, they are probably going to be looking at their tweets themselves, answering them themselves and generally getting involved. As time goes on and Twitter becomes ubiquitous this, of course, will change. Those in high places will become overwhelmed by the number of personal tweets they receive and they will farm the whole thing out to a management team and the whole point of Twitter will be lost. But right now, its ability to put you in direct contact with people and bypass all their layers of PAs and gatekeepers in the process is remarkable. Make the most of it while you can.

I decided to test Twitter's real power by sending out a tweet while writing this chapter. At 7.48pm one Saturday evening I sent out this tweet:

Anyone know how to take a screen grab of a webpage pls? I want to get a page of my site Entrepreneurthings. com for a speech #asktwitter.

Adding the hashtag (#) asktwitter meant that anyone typing in #asktwitter would see my tweet. Within minutes I had received replies from fifteen people I didn't know, all telling me exactly how to do it. Amazing. (In case you were wondering, you need to press FN and the print screen key (PRTSC) on your keyboard at the same time – this copies the page you are looking at, even though, ridiculously, it doesn't actually tell you it has done it. Then all you need to do is open a new Word document and paste it into it. Who knew?)

Kate Jenkins is such an enthusiast she has effectively built her entire business through Twitter. She started out in 2007 making chocolate brownies in the kitchen of her cottage in Llanmabog in the Gower Peninsula, Wales, which she sold in the local village shop. People loved them and when she started winning awards for her brownies she spent £200 creating a basic website and began to sell them online, posting out her brownies via Royal Mail in boxes of sixteen.

A year later a friend suggested that Kate join Twitter to promote her venture. Initially she was resistant but she signed up anyway as @gowercottage and started running a competition each week, the prize being a box of her brownies. The competition was never actually about brownies – it would always be something funny or silly, such as suggesting the best chat-up line for Valentine's Day, or imagining what song might be playing in the changing room at a rugby match. The brownies would go to people tweeting the best answer. Her 'Monday Mayhem' competitions quickly built up a following, to the extent that Kate would often find herself trending on Twitter – in other words being one of the most popular topics.

More than 69,000 tweets later, Kate now has nearly 5,000 followers, and the turnover of her business has risen to

£120,000, of which she estimates £40,000 has come entirely via Twitter. Votes from her followers also helped her win the Observer Food Monthly award for Best Welsh online retailer two years in a row.

Kate says: 'It is not just that people are buying my brownies, they are also supporting me and doing PR for me because they are talking about my brownies. Twitter is like the biggest word of mouth.'

You do, however, have to work out fairly quickly whether Twitter is actually integral to you getting more sales for your business, as in Kate's case, or whether it is just a way of publicising it. If the first, then it is worth spending time on; if the second, not so much. Tweeting for tweeting's sake takes up time you could be spending on other areas of your venture.

You also have to treat Twitter with care and respect. Twitter is a business tool and should be used as such. Remember, tweets live for ever. You can delete them from your own account but they will live on till the end of time in someone else's computer. I was surprised to see a tweet from someone I know in a professional capacity recently which said she had just embarked on a new diet and had lost lots of weight. Noooooo. I really didn't need to know that.

Facebook and YouTube

Two other ways of promoting your business for free online are via Facebook (Facebook.com) and YouTube (Youtube.com). On Facebook you can create a page for your business, on which you can post information, offers, photos, details of forthcoming events and so on. Simply click on the 'create a page' button on the home page. You will be given six options to choose from, of which three are somewhat overlapping business-related options. You can opt to be categorised as a local business or place; a company, organisation or institution; or a brand or product. After some deliberation I choose the category 'brand or product' for Entrepreneurthings.com. I then upload a picture of a mug (badly – only a bit of it fits into the box provided – I still can't decide whether this looks cool or silly) and am asked to provide some information about the product, which I do. Finally, I need to choose a unique Facebook web address – so I get http://www.facebook.com/Entrepreneurthings. That's it – in the space of a minute or two the page is set up, and I can start to invite my friends and email contacts to 'like' the page, and update the page status to share news with visitors.

A Facebook page can be an effective way of creating a focal point for your business where customers can go and instantly find out what's 'going on'. So it obviously works best for those businesses which actually do have something interesting going on, and on a regular basis – new products being launched, new places where the products are being sold, the dates of local fairs or events where customers can come and meet you in person, and so on. If your business doesn't actually have much of interest to share with customers – if it's a consultancy, say, and you need to keep client names confidential or your customers are not the type of people likely to frequent Facebook – then it will have limited value. Plus it's important to remember that while it works a bit like your own mini website, there is a big difference – in this case it is not 'your' site, it remains part of Facebook and so is subject to whatever controls and rules Facebook may decide to impose.

YouTube allows you to upload videos about your venture for free so potential customers can see them. The best way to get your business noticed is to create a dedicated YouTube Channel for it – effectively a page on YouTube just for your business. I manage to create an Entrepreneur Things channel – it's at http://www.youtube.com/user/Entrepreneurthings – and change the picture and the background colour. Now all I have to do is make some videos of famous people drinking tea from my mugs and upload them . . .

One more networking site to mention. Linkedin (linkedin. com) is basically an online address book – it's a useful way of being able to find and contact people in their professional world. As with Twitter, Facebook, YouTube and so on, the same rules for all apply. Dip a toe in, see if it benefits your business in any tangible way, limit the time you spend on it, and, above all, don't get obsessed. Social networks are useful, but they are only part of the marketing and promotion picture.

Going viral

There's one aspect of social networking which is incredibly powerful and exciting but which is impossible to plan or predict. And that is when an idea goes viral. In other words, when it suddenly attracts massive attention and develops a life of its own.

When Adam King decided to propose to his girlfriend

Lucy on the 19.57 train from Euston to Watford, he decided to enlist the help of some friends. Unbeknown to Lucy, when she and Adam boarded the train, so too did twenty-five members of the amateur choir Adam belonged to. They were strategically placed around the carriage and when the train started moving they burst into song, singing 'Lovely Day' by Bill Withers. When they had finished Adam got down on one knee and asked a rather surprised Lucy to marry him. Fortunately, she said yes. Some of the people taking part videoed the event on their mobile phones so Adam could put it on YouTube to share with everyone he knew.

He says: 'The idea was we would ring people and tell them to go on YouTube, and we would stay on the phone and listen to their reaction as they watched it. It was a really fun way of telling people we were engaged.'

But that was not all that happened. One of his friends tweeted about it and the story was picked up by the London *Evening Standard* newspaper which ran a piece about it on their front page. That piece was picked up by the *Sun* and the *Daily Mail*, both of which ran the story the following morning. Before he knew it, Adam's YouTube video was being viewed by people all round the world. It had gone viral.

America's ABC News got in touch and ran a piece about them. So did CBS, whose piece went live to ten million people in the US. The *London Tonight* television show ran a piece. Adam and Lucy suddenly found themselves in demand from media outlets from around the world. Indeed, the global interest was so intense that Adam had to set up a media centre in his flat and abandon all other work for a week while he dealt with enquiries.

He says: 'The phone just went bananas. It was an amazing experience.'

There have been other knock-on benefits, too. Even though the video had nothing to do with the tailoring operation which Adam had co-founded, King and Allen, it too benefited by association – not in actual sales, but in generating a good feeling among existing customers.

Adam says: 'We have 18,000 customers and half of them saw the video. It basically made King and Allen look like a really nice place to do business with.'

The YouTube clip has now been seen more than 2.5 million times. Meanwhile the choir, the Adam Street Singers, have been inundated with applications from people hoping to join, and have been booked for their first corporate gig.

Getting into print

One of the cheapest and most effective ways of telling the world about you and your business is to get a newspaper or magazine to write about you in a feature or news story. Not only will the piece be read by the readers themselves, it is also likely to be read by other journalists, who may decide they want to write about you in their newspaper or magazine too. Or it may even be read by researchers looking for stories to feature on local television news programmes.

The good news is you don't need to spend a fortune on hiring a public relations consultant to do it for you; you can do it yourselves and it will cost absolutely nothing (sorry PR people). Here's how:

▶▶ Do your homework. Read the business sections of each newspaper, and the relevant trade magazines, carefully to find out which journalists write about small businesses and entrepreneurs. This may sound blindingly obvious but you would be amazed at how many PR people – who really should know better – just blindly fire off emails at random in the hope that one of them might strike gold. They don't. Ideally you want to draw up a list of, say, half a dozen journalists who might be interested in your story and then contact each of them in turn. And don't forget online publications, too – many trade magazines in particular have become purely internet-based operations in recent years, but are still widely read.

▶▶ Decide what the story is. Why would a journalist be interested in writing about you? And why now? It might be that your business has just done something newsworthy – won an award, perhaps, or been awarded a contract that had been expected to go to a much larger company. Or it might be that you yourself are the story, perhaps because of the unusual way you set up the business. If you are not sure what your story is, then ask people close to you what they think. The story angle may change depending on whether it is for local or national press – regional newspapers will understandably be more interested in a local angle. However, a word of warning – don't try to add colour just for the sake of it. There is nothing more infuriating than ringing someone up who you have been told works from a cow shed at the bottom of the garden only to discover that a) it is not really a cow shed at all, and b) they only worked there for one day while their office was being redecorated.

▶▶ Send an email and keep it short and to the point. If you are contacting a journalist on a national newspaper don't bother writing a press release, because that makes it look like you have sent it to lots of people (which you shouldn't be doing anyway) and so is likely to be ignored. Instead, email the journalist direct, addressing her or him by name – try not to send it to 'the news editor', or 'the features editor' unless you have to – saying what your business does and why it is interesting and how they can contact you. Journalists have very short attention spans and very large inboxes so you need to grab their interest in the first line or the moment will be lost. If the switchboard won't tell you the journalist's email address then just guess – it is likely to be *firstname.lastname@newspaper.co.uk*. Ringing them instead of emailing is a high-risk strategy and not recommended – you are bound to pick the moment when the journalist is close to deadline, they will sound cross and won't be concentrating on what you are saying, and your moment will be lost. The only exception to the 'no press release' rule is if you are contacting your local paper – many are sadly under-resourced nowadays so may appreciate a succinct press release with a quote and some background context, and even a photo. Again, keep it simple and clear so it is obvious what the story is about. And don't bother trying to write the story yourself in the style of the newspaper – apparently some public relations courses advise people to do this, but it is complete a waste of time. It feels rather patronising and it's bound to come out wrong. After all, writing the story is the journalist's job. Just tell them the facts in one sentence and they'll do the rest.

▶▶ Be honest. Your aim is to build a relationship of trust with the journalist so that they will want to follow the progress of your business and write about you again. So if another paper has written about your company recently, or interviewed you for a piece which has not yet been published, say so. They still might want to write about you, but with a different angle. And if you don't and the journalist ends up looking foolish because the piece has already appeared elsewhere, then it's goodbye to your new friendship.

ACTION PLAN

▶▶ Spend a morning creating a Facebook page and signing up to Twitter and Linkedin – and possibly Google Plus if you are feeling enthusiastic. If you would like to, practise by sending me a tweet to say hello – I'm on @rachelbridge100.

▶▶ Start slowly – aim to post two tweets a week and to update your Facebook page once a week. Linkedin will run itself – just respond to emails requesting that you link to others as they appear.

▶▶ Spend a day in your local library – and online – drawing up a list of all the publications and journalists that might be interested in writing about you and your business.

CHAPTER 13

HOW TO SPEND NOTHING ON ADVERTISING

When Christina Lundberg and Rustan Panday launched their online business Bed Of Nails selling acupressure mats known as bed of nails, they knew that the only way customers would find their website would be if it appeared at the top of the free natural search results on the first page of Google, the search engine, whenever someone typed in the phrase 'bed of nails'. That way, potential customers would see their website first – and so hopefully buy their products rather than those of their competitors.

So they got to work using search engine optimisation (SEO) techniques to encourage Google to notice their website, and then they backed this up with a bit of search engine marketing (SEM), running occasional low-cost, pay-per-click adverts down the side of Google's search results page.

Their efforts paid off. Within six months of launching their business in 2009, Christina and Rustan had managed to get their website to the top of Google's natural search results, meaning that every time a customer typed in a search for 'bed of nails', their website would come top of the list. As a result sales of their acupressure mats have soared, with online sales accounting for 40 per cent of total sales. Their mats are also stocked in Harvey Nichols and Fenwick, with customers buying them to relieve everything from back pain to insomnia.

Christina says: 'What I discovered is that there is a whole science behind search engine optimisation. You can do it on a very basic level or you can do it on an advanced level, and you can improve it all the time. It is becoming increasingly essential because, if you don't do it, somebody else will.'

There is no point in creating a fantastic website selling wonderful products if nobody can find it. Sadly, it is no longer enough simply to 'put it out there' and hope for the best. With more than 250 million websites in existence worldwide, even the smallest business needs to do a bit of search engine optimisation if it is to stand a chance of being noticed.

SEO is basically the art of persuading search engines such as Google to put you somewhere near the top of their natural list of suggested websites when someone types in a request which you could fulfil. If you sell dog baskets, for example, your life will be made a whole lot easier – and your business a whole lot more successful – if your website comes out top of the list every time someone types the words 'dog baskets' into the search engine.

But first, a quick lesson on different types of search results. If you look carefully at a Google search page you will see the first few results are enclosed in a light pink box, with the words 'Ads – why these ads?' written in the top left-hand – or sometimes top right-hand – corner. The websites listed here have paid to be here – they are not there because they are most relevant to your search. They might still be useful, but it is the results immediately below the pink box that we are interested in right now, because those are the free natural listings as decided by Google.

There is a good reason why everyone wants their website to appear near the top of free listings: websites which appear in the top three places of a search engine's natural – as opposed to paid-for – results attract an astonishing 98 per cent of the traffic for that particular search, while the website in first place attracts a whopping 60 per cent of the traffic all by itself. As you probably know from your own experience, even though a search can generate millions of results – a search for dog baskets produces 22.4 million websites to choose from, for example – people very rarely bother to look at the second results page or beyond. In fact, they often don't even bother to scroll down to see the bottom of the first page.

Getting to the top of the natural list, however, does not just happen by chance. You have to work at it. Exactly how Google decides to rank the websites on its natural search list is a closely guarded secret, based on algorithms which are constantly being tweaked. But what we do know is that the results are displayed according to how relevant Google feels they are to what you are looking for. The key word to focus on here is relevant. Google's algorithm searchers

– known as spiders – constantly trawl through the millions of websites out there to find what it feels are the most relevant sites to a search request.

Relevancy is determined by several factors such as the content of your website – both visible and embedded – how many other sites link to yours, how many people visit the site and how often the content on your website is updated. Other factors, such as how long the website has been running for, are also taken into account.

Your job is to try and show Google's spiders that your site is the most relevant site for the terms being searched for. And that means being proactive.

So how do you go about it?

1. Meta tags

First, you need to build meta tags into the fabric of your website. Meta tags are words which you can write into the html code of your website – in other words the unseen instruction part of your website. They can't be seen by people looking at your website but they are recognised by Google and other search engines as they trawl the internet looking for relevant sites.

They should indicate to the Google spiders what your website is about by using key words which describe its contents. The meta tags on my Entrepreneur Things website, for example, include mug, entrepreneur, pink, ceramic, tea and coffee. That means if you type in 'entrepreneur' and 'mug' into Google, the spiders will find my site, realise it is relevant, and – hopefully – put my Entrepreneur Things website among the top few natural search listings.

The good news is that Google has provided lots of free online tools to help you get to grips with all this. Your first stop should be Google Analytics (google.com/analytics) which will tell you about the performance of your website – how many people visit it, which pages they look at and for how long. It is actually quite mind-boggling just how much information it can give you. Google Webmaster Tools (google.com/webmaster) will show you how to make your website as search-engine friendly as possible to maximise its visibility on the internet.

2. Content

Second, you need to include the words and phrases you wish to be known for into the content of your website, regularly and consistently. If you are selling angora jumpers, for example, then always describe them as 'angora jumpers' rather than angora tops, say, or woollen jumpers.

Because there is so much competition out there, however, the chances of your website being noticed by the Google spiders – and therefore put high up the natural search list – will be hugely improved if you can find yourself a niche, by highlighting any unusual or specialist products which you sell.

As a small start-up you basically have no chance of being listed on the first page of a search engine for popular single- or even two-word mainstream products because you are in competition with much larger firms which will be seen by

Google as being far more relevant. You may be selling cordless kettles, for example, but so, too, are Debenhams and Robert Dyas. And they have far bigger selling clout and far more customers than you do clicking on their website and so they will always beat you in a natural search selection.

So you need to highlight products for which there will be less competition on the web. If your website sells products for hikers and outdoor walkers, for example, then you will get a lot more attention if you highlight, say, the head torches you sell than if you highlight walking boots, because there will be far fewer sites selling head torches than walking boots. You should also include the words head torches into your website's meta tags.

Another way of doing this is to be very specific in your description of your products. While there will be many websites selling picnic blankets, there will be far fewer selling pink tartan picnic blankets, for example.

As you can see, it's an art rather than a science – you need to strike a balance between choosing keywords which are so specialised that hardly anyone is searching for them, and those which are so popular that the weight of competition will squeeze you out.

The good news is there is a free tool to help to decide which words will attract the most customers. Google's free search keyword tool (go to adwords.google.com and then click on 'Tools and Analysis' then keyword 'Tool') will tell you exactly how many people were using particular search terms to find things on the internet in the past month.

Typing in the phrase 'plastic garden sheds', for example, reveals that 5,400 people in the UK were looking for these in an average month over the past year, compared with 2,900 people who were looking for wooden garden sheds.

By tweaking the words you put in your website to match the things which potential customers are actually looking for – and, indeed, by adjusting your actual product range to fit their needs – you hugely improve your chance of getting online sales. If you sell yellow polka-dot bikinis, for example, you might think your keywords should be 'yellow polka-dot bikinis'. But if nobody has ever searched for 'yellow polka-dot bikinis' in the past year, then making that a key focus for your website would prevent customers finding your site. It would be better to highlight some other niche product that people do actually search for.

3. Links

Get other well-regarded sites to mention your site and to include a link to it. The simplest place to start is to create a Facebook page and Twitter account for your business which link to your site. Links from a trade organisation or local community website are useful, too. You might also be able to get bloggers to link to your site, perhaps by sending them some products to review. And you should definitely write a regular blog yourself on your website – basically a regularly updated online newsletter – which people can follow and link to. It is not only a great way to stay in touch with your customers; it also is a good way of constantly updating the content of your website and so ensuring that the Google spiders find you.

Another option is to link the content of your Twitter feed

to your website, so that every time you put out a message on Twitter it automatically appears in a continually updated box on the home page of your website. Personally, though, I think doing this can look a bit weird. By its very nature, Twitter-speak is truncated and abbreviated and it can be hard to read out of Twitter-land and out of context. A better option is to filter the messages so that only the really useful ones appear on your website.

Search engine marketing

The main problem with trying to boost your natural ranking on Google is that it is time-consuming and will not happen overnight – it typically takes a new business between six months and a year for its SEO efforts to pay off in the shape of improved ranking, partly because new websites are automatically given a lower rating by Google than established ones and partly because things like blogs and links take time to be noticed.

So in the early stages of starting up you might also want to consider supplementing your SEO efforts with some SEM – search engine marketing. Otherwise known as PPC, or pay-per-click advertising – and known on Google as Google Adwords. (I've focused on Google as it's the biggest and most used search engine but other search engines operate in much the same way.)

Google Adwords are the square little advert boxes which pop up on the screen to the right-hand side of the natural search listings. They appear when someone types the relevant keywords – as decided by you – into the search engine. The idea is you only pay a fee if someone is sufficiently interested in your advert to click on it. That then takes them straight through to your website – or, even better, to the page of your website which you have decided is most relevant, for example the product page rather than the home page.

It is at about this point that suddenly the thought of having a real-life, on-the-ground, touch-and-feel market stall or pop-up shop seems incredibly appealing. Hello, real customers, here are my real products for you to see: what would you like to buy? But you must be brave and bold. The online marketplace is going to become increasingly important as customers migrate to the internet, so even if you decide SEM is not for you, you do need to know what it does and why, not least because your competitors may well be using it. So let's press on.

The big benefit of SEM for start-ups is that, unlike SEO, which takes time to come into effect, you can start using pay-per-click advertising straight away. The downside is that pay-per-click adverts cost a bit of money, although not a lot – depending on the words you want to target, a couple of pounds a day might be sufficient.

I decide it's time for me to start using a bit of SEM to tell the world about my entrepreneur mugs. I go to Google Adwords (adwords.google.co.uk) and open an account – I already have a Google email account so that bit's easy. The Google Adwords website is fascinating and daunting in equal measure. There are tabs called Campaigns, Opportunities and Tools and Analysis. I love the way they call it a campaign.

It sounds so important and exciting. There is also a graph which at the moment is flatlining but will presumably swing into action when my campaign does.

I manage to write an advert after several attempts to get the words to fit into the box provided. It reads: 'Mugs for entrepreneurs. Lovely mugs which say ENTREPRENEUR. The perfect present. www.entrepreneurthings.com'. Then I realise it would be better to put the price of my mugs in my advert so people know what to expect when they click on it. If I'm paying for every time someone clicks on my advert I might as well get rid of the time-wasters in advance before they cost me any money. So I change it to 'The perfect present for £10'. The next step is to decide on my keywords. These are the words which will trigger the advert to appear.

The trick here is to strike the right balance – if the keywords are too popular they will a) cost you a lot of money, and b) not get you very high up the column of adverts that appear. The price per click is determined by an auction process, with sought-after keywords costing more than less popular words. The cost per click typically ranges from 25p to £2, though the phrase 'credit card' has soared to £15, showing how much in demand it is.

It's a novel way of looking at the whole marketing issue because it forces you to think how much you are prepared to spend acquiring each individual sale. There is no point spending 50p per click, for example, if an actual sale will only make you a profit of 50p.

When I start to put in keywords for my website I initially don't realise you can include phrases as well as single words so I put down 'mugs' 'entrepreneurs' 'gifts' and 'inspiring'. Google Adwords doesn't seem very impressed with my selection, however, because when I press enter it tells me that some of my words are 'rarely shown due to low-quality score'. This is written in red so I get the message that this is definitely not a good thing. Fortunately they are easy to delete.

Then I choose a daily maximum budget limit which I want to spend. If it costs me 40p every time someone clicks on my advert then £2 a day will get me five clicks. When the budget is reached, the advert doesn't appear again that day.

There is another problem. Google Adwords doesn't like me putting the word ENTREPRENEUR in capitals, even though this is how it appears on the mugs. I can ask for it to be considered for a special exception, which I do, but the next day they email me with bad news. The email reads: 'After reviewing your account, we found that one or more of your ads or keywords have been disapproved. Until you edit your ads or keywords to make them compliant, your ads unfortunately won't be able to show up on Google, our search partners or on Display Network placements.'

The good thing about Google Adwords is they know it is all going to be a bit overwhelming at first. The next day I get a nice email from them saying I can call for free support for the next six weeks, and, when I telephone them a week later, Barry on the other end tells me I can call him as often as I want in that time. He also promises to take another look at the whole ENTREPRENEUR/entrepreneur thing and get back to me, and he suggests some improvements to my keywords – namely that I can use phrases not just words and I can list up to 500 of them. That's an enormous number. I struggled to get past six. Barry is quite complimentary about my advert, saying I've been attracting four or five clicks a day, in other words up to my limit. Shame none of them have actually bought a mug as a result.

I call Rob Hill, who founded The Stag Company, an online business which organises pre-wedding holidays and weekends away for the groom and friends. He tells me that all his business comes through search engine optimisation and pay-per-click Google Adwords.

I try it out, typing 'stag weekend business' into Google. Sure enough, his website pops up first on the free natural search selection and sixth on the paid for pay-per-click adverts down the side.

Rob started the operation ten years ago with £15,000 borrowed on credit cards. His firm, which is based in Brighton, now has a turnover of £7.5 million and employs forty people.

It almost ended in disaster before it had even begun, however. Having got to grips with PPC – or so he thought – Rob spent £1,000 buying keywords for his adverts, and then sat back and waited for the calls to come. But nothing happened. After three days he had not received a single enquiry.

By then he was in a panic. He says: 'I was just thinking, oh my God, what have I done?' When he called Google to find out what was going on, they told him to try out the pay-per-click link himself – at which point Rob discovered he had misspelt the link so no one was actually being put through to his website.

He fixed the link and got his first booking three weeks later, worth £1,500. He says: 'I was just bouncing around the office.' The moral of the story is – first check that your Adword actually works.

I get an email from Barry at Adwords support. He tells me my request to put the word 'ENTREPRENEUR' in caps in my advert has been rejected – again – because it 'violates their capitalisation policy'.

He writes: 'We do not allow ads with excessive or gimmicky capitalization, regardless of whether it is the name of the product you are advertising or not. Thank you for your understanding and co-operation with this issue.'

Ah well. I go back into my Google Adwords account and change ENTREPRENEUR to entrepreneur. Then, for good measure, I play around with my key words. Out goes 'gifts', in comes 'entrepreneur gifts'. Out goes 'inspiring' and in comes 'inspiring gifts'. These are the tweaks which will make me my millions. Then, feeling emboldened, I increase my daily budget limit from £2 to £2.50. Oh yes. There's no stopping me now.

I try typing 'entrepreneur mugs' into Google and, yes, there it is – my little advert, right at the top of the column on the right-hand side. I am ridiculously pleased. Then, remembering Rob Hill's advice, I click on it to test it actually works. It takes me straight through to the product page on my website and there are my mugs. Hooray: 40p well spent.

Well, sort of. A few weeks later Google Adwords kindly emails me a progress report of my account's performance.

It tells me that just 0.09 per cent of the people who see my advert – and, remember, these are the people who are presumably actively looking for entrepreneur mugs, because otherwise they wouldn't get to see my advert in the first place – actually click on my advert and go through to my website. 0.09 per cent. That means of the 74,823 people who have seen my advert, only sixty-six of them actually bothered to click on it.

Finally, a warning. You need to keep on top of your Adword campaigns. Watch how they are doing and what business they are bringing in. Do not just leave them to run and forget about them, as I did. Even though I had set my budget to a tiny £2.50 a day – and even reduced it to £1.50 a day at one point – by the time I checked back in with Google Adwords to see what was going on I realised I had spent £34.04 in November, £29.06 in December, £33.11 in January and £12.61 in February – a staggering total of £108.82, which had brought in a handful of mugs orders at best. I was stunned and felt quite sick. It was too much money to be spending on something which clearly wasn't working in the way it should be. So set a limit to your campaign, watch it like a hawk, and if it doesn't seem to be working then change the parameters until it does.

ACTION PLAN

▶▶ Start writing a blog on your website. It doesn't have to be long – 200 words will do. Use it to tell your customers what your business is doing and invite feedback by email. Update it every two weeks.

▶▶ Never use an ampersand (&) as part of your business name – you can't put it in your website address so will have to use 'and' instead, causing endless confusion for your customers and making it impossible for the Google spiders to find you.

▶▶ Set up a Google Adword account and run a test campaign for a week. Check the data every day to see how many people are clicking on your advert and which words are attracting them – and which are not.

CHAPTER 14

HOW TO GET FREE HELP AND ADVICE

The email is blunt. It reads: 'I know it is still a work in progress but although I could order a pink mug I had to close the shopping cart window to try and add a blue mug and I couldn't then reconnect to the shopping cart. Also I didn't know the price of the mugs until I got to the cart and then it wasn't clear whether the £2.50 postage was for one mug or would cover two mugs if I ordered both? Then I tried to email you through the link to enquiries given on the site but it would not let me send you a message. Thought other people may have the same problem?'

The email is from my mother and it isn't exactly the kind of email I want to receive. But as an impartial and frank

– and free – assessment of my fledgling Enterpreneur Things website, it is worth its weight in gold.

Used wisely, feedback is one of the most useful tools available to a business, which is why practically every big company seems to be completely obsessed with it right now. You can't do anything these days without a feedback form popping up ten minutes later telling you that Big Corporate values your opinion and would like to hear your views, and please could you take a few minutes to click here and complete their online survey. A quick perusal of my email account reveals that I have been asked my opinion on numerous occasions by companies from Asda to PayPal.

Or, as Asda puts it:

Dear Customer,

At ASDA, we value the opinions of our customers. As we strive to continually improve on the level of service we provide, we would like to hear your feed-back regarding your recent interaction with our colleague.

We ask that you take a few minutes of your time to complete our online survey. Your insight and opinions will help us serve you better in the future.

Please click here to complete our brief online survey.

Sometimes the company which is asking for your opinion, sensibly guessing that we might be fast approaching feedback fatigue, will try to sweeten the experience by promising to enter you into a competition. Q Hotels, the owner of the Nottingham Belfry hotel, for example, promised that completing their survey would give me the chance to win a two-night weekend stay for two at one of their hotels.

Emails are quite easy to ignore, thankfully. Much worse are the companies who ring you up after you have at last managed to get through to speak to a real person at your electricity provider or broadband provider, or whatever.

Big Corporate: 'How was your experience of your phone call with us?'

Me: 'Eh? What? I've just spent twenty-five minutes on the phone trying to get through to you, and now YOU call ME? How about diverting some of your feedback phone call people to answering the phone when customers actually call you in need of help? Please go away now.'

My friend Paul was even asked for his feedback by the undertakers organising the funeral of his mother.

Used carefully and wisely, though, feedback can be an extremely useful tool for entrepreneurs starting out. You may not agree with what people say, but even that in itself can be useful as it makes you think about why you don't agree with what they said, and what, indeed, you do think about the issue in question.

I occasionally help successful entrepreneurs write

books about their experiences; the way it works is they write it all down, and then I read it and tell them which bits are interesting, which bits are boring and irrelevant, which bits make sense and which don't. I tend to get the red pen out, for example, for too much detailed description about which schools they went to, or their former jobs, unless they shed some revealing light on how they have turned out subsequently.

On the other hand, I'm very keen on the bits which reveal – subconsciously or otherwise – some real insight into what makes the entrepreneur tick. I mark the changes I would make on the Word document, then send it back to the entrepreneur for them to accept or reject as they see fit. Occasionally this can lead to some highly entertaining exchanges, as we bat chapters to and fro, amid utter outrage on the part of the entrepreneur about some choice phrase or hilarious anecdote which I have red-inked as irrelevant and in need of removing. But the great thing about having someone to look over your work critically is that even if you choose to ignore what they suggest, it does at least force you to think hard about why you feel that way.

Ask the right person

Of course it is important you seek feedback from the right person. Don't ask someone who knows nothing about fashion to comment on the kind of clothes you are planning to sell. The reason entrepreneurs ask me for my help with their books is because they trust me to do a good job

– because I have written about them in the past while Enterprise Editor of the *Sunday Times*; because I am a journalist so I know how to tell a story; and because I am the author of several books myself. Another advantage is that because I am not personally involved in their story I can be an impartial observer and look at it in a clear, detached way.

When I launched my Entrepreneur Things website I sent an email with the website link to a friend I know and trust, who has also just started his own venture. He responded immediately and helpfully with a lot of useful thoughts that I could work through and think about. Thanks, James.

One way of formalising the feedback process and getting free advice at the same time is to find yourself a mentor; someone who can offer advice, contacts and the wisdom of experience. A mentoring arrangement can take many forms, from an occasional phone call to a regular structured meeting. Though it may involve payment to the mentor for his or her time, in the UK it is far more common for it to be an unpaid arrangement.

The key element defining the relationship is that the mentor is there to offer informed, objective advice and support based on his or her experience, with the aim of increasing the other person's chances of success.

When Ged Backland was a young, inexperienced designer, he was guided and advised by an industry veteran called Ralph Shaffer, who explained how to shape his ideas and how the industry worked.

Ged, who now runs his own successful enterprise, the Backland Studio, in Haworth, West Yorkshire, never forgot Ralph's generosity and now mentors young people himself.

'For me it is about giving somebody else a chance,' he says. 'Ralph took me under his wing and taught me everything I know and I have gone on to become very successful. So if I can do that for somebody else it bodes well for good karma and creativity. I get great satisfaction from seeing people realise their potential.'

For a mentoring relationship to work well, however, there has to be something in it for the mentor, too. A purely one-way relationship in which the mentor always gives and the person being mentored always takes will not last. Ged, who has created characters such as GoochiCoo and the Suga Lumps for greetings cards and marketing campaigns, says he gets something out of the arrangement as well.

He says: 'Mentoring inspires me. The people I mentor are creative forces in their own right and I learn from them, too, because they come into the profession without any preconceived ideas.'

Gérard Basset, owner of Hotel TerraVina in the New Forest, Hampshire, has been a wine and business mentor for twenty years. He says: 'I have learnt a lot by mentoring. It is not a one-way street – every time you mentor you learn from your students. For me, mentoring anyone who has a genuine passion can be extremely rewarding.'

Mentoring a chef, of course, comes with particular benefits – his protégés, who include Xavier Rousset, the co-owner of Texture, a Michelin-starred restaurant in London's Marylebone, often pay in kind with meals at their restaurants.

The problem with mentoring, however, is:

▶▶ it can be really hard to find a mentor

▶▶ it can be difficult to ask someone to give up so much of their time

▶▶ you only get one person's advice, no matter how good it is

The good news is there is a wonderful free – and brilliantly simple – solution to this:

Go informal

Create an informal panel of advisers for your business, who meet on a regular basis to provide advice and constructive criticism. That way you get several points of view, and it is a much less onerous commitment for everyone involved. This is exactly what Anthony Alderson has done.

Anthony, the director of The Pleasance, a charitable trust which runs some of the best known venues at the Edinburgh festival plus a theatre in North London, is bursting with ideas but he knows not all of them can be pursued at the same time. And indeed that some of them might be unworkable or downright bonkers. So to help him decide which ideas to follow first, he has gathered together an informal group of external advisers to guide and challenge him, as well as share their experience and provide expertise. There are currently six members on the panel – which is separate from the board of trustees which governs The Pleasance – including a theatre director, a musician, an IT expert, a financial adviser, and me. We meet for two hours after work every three months in a room at The Pleasance, fortified by wine and often followed by dinner in the pub.

For Anthony, the development board gives him a safe and supportive environment in which he can suggest ideas, however outlandish. For the members of the board it can provide a fascinating insight into a company or organisation they support, and a chance to help it forge a way forward.

As Anthony says: 'The development board is a place where I can come up with lunatic ideas and not feel like I am being a nitwit. The point of it is to provide a sounding board for me, both as an artistic director and as chief executive. No organisation can afford to sit still. You have to keep moving constantly.'

It is a model which would work well for start-ups because it provides a win-win arrangement for both sides. The entrepreneur gets access to a range of free expert advice, views and opinions; the panel members get to be involved in something in which they can make a real difference. And, crucially, the time commitment for them is much less onerous than being a mentor. I don't get paid for being on the development board of The Pleasance, but I feel very privileged to be involved with an organisation that I hugely respect and admire, and through it I have met some fascinating people.

Keith Hunt is the managing partner of Results International, a consultancy which has also created its own sounding board

– an informal group of 'friends' who share their wisdom every few months over a good dinner.

He says: 'It can be lonely being an entrepreneur. You find yourself having to make decisions left, right and centre, often about things you have no real experience of, and you can feel pretty exposed. It is easy to lose perspective. So it is extremely important to have a group of experienced people whom you can call on and who can keep you in check, as well as giving you some sound advice.'

Daniel Priestley also decided to create an informal panel of advisers to support Triumphant Events, his training and promotions company. He found it so helpful he now helps put together external advisory boards for other small firms.

He says: 'When you are running a new business you are often too close to it to see the value you are sitting on. It is like standing on a mountain – you can't tell the size or shape of it because you are too close. It takes someone who is off the mountain to tell you what it looks like.'

Listen to yourself

One thing, though – always taste-test advice and figure out for yourself if it's actually right for you. And don't discount the value of your own opinions and thoughts, because they count for a lot. Not long ago I gave my sister some memorable advice on how to parallel park – in other words, for those who have the luxury of living outside London and are unfamiliar with the concept – how to back your car into a very small parking space along a street when there doesn't look as if there is enough room. 'There is always a lot more room than you think between you and the car behind you,' I said loftily. 'Just keep going back.' Well, she remembered these pearls of wisdom the next time she was parallel parking and against her better judgement followed my advice – and as it turned out, there wasn't more room than she thought after all. Oops.

Co-habit

Another way of getting free advice and help is simply to locate your business in the same place as other ventures operating in the same industry. This is what is happening in Shoreditch, east London, a once rundown area of London which has been nicknamed Silicon Roundabout because of its high concentration of high-tech start-ups.

Michael Acton-Smith moved his computer game firm Mind Candy, best known for its game Moshi Monsters, across the city from Battersea in the south at the beginning of 2011, lured by the idea of being surrounded by similarly minded fast-growing technology developers.

He explains why: 'We are hiring incredibly quickly and we felt the best place to be would be Shoreditch because there are so many similar firms around here and there is a great after-work scene. I love chatting to other entrepreneurs running similar businesses because there is so much we share – how we find new employees, what salaries we are paying, who is raising money.'

Michael has even started up Silicon Drinkabout, an

informal gathering in a pub every Friday night where workers from local firms can come together and share news and gossip over a drink.

The great thing about being in the same place as everyone else is it makes it easy to take advantage of shared knowledge, pools of skilled labour and networking opportunities. Often ideas are hatched simply by bumping into people in the common spaces – on the pavement or in the coffee shop.

Consider incubation

Telefonica has taken this idea one step further with the establishment of Wayra, an incubator in central London aimed at technology based start-ups. An incubator is essentially a low-cost, supportive environment designed to help and encourage new businesses to thrive. Entrepreneurs who are accepted on to the Wayra programme, for example, receive free workspace, coaching and mentoring for six months, plus 50,000 euros. In return, Telefonica takes a 10 per cent equity stake in their venture.

Meanwhile, in Nottingham, a former pharmaceutical research facility has become Bio City, home and incubator to seventy small life-science ventures which benefit enormously from sharing advice and help with each other.

As well as getting low-cost office and laboratory space, the companies based in Bio City also benefit from pay-per-use access to expensive research equipment they could never afford to buy on their own.

It means small start-ups benefit not only from the pool of talented workers; they can also offer staff many of the benefits of a much larger company – from industry networking and training to five-a-side football teams and yoga sessions.

Glenn Crocker, chief executive of Bio City, believes that shared work spaces such as his offer immense benefits to small start-ups, not least the networking possibilities. He says: 'Even the stairwell is an important networking point here. It can take twenty minutes to get up two flights of stairs because you are talking to people on the way.'

The other advantage is that by clustering together in this way, small firms can make a much bigger splash than a small company could on its own. Glenn says: 'Investors can come up from London and have a look at five or ten companies all in one go, and that makes them more likely to do it.'

You can, of course, also get a great deal of help and advice from your own potential customers. When Sally Robinson decided she wanted to sell bras for women with bigger busts, she simply stood in the centre of York for a day and stopped passers-by – choosing women who she thought might be in need of a larger bra – to ask them what they thought of the idea.

While some were understandably shy about talking to a stranger about their underwear, others readily confirmed what she instinctively believed: there were plenty of potential customers unable to find big bras on the high street. Sally did some more research into the size of the market and who her competitors would be. Then she took the plunge and now runs Ample Bosom from the family farm in North Yorkshire with six staff, selling hundreds of bras a month in sizes from 28A to 58J.

ACTION PLAN

▶▶ Draw up a list of specific areas where you would find external advice useful.

▶▶ Compile a list of five people you would like to join an informal advisory board for your business. Now invite them.

▶▶ Set an agenda for every meeting and circulate beforehand. Always end the meeting on time; informal discussions can always continue over drinks later.

CHAPTER 15

THE IMPORTANCE OF STARTING SMALL

I've started my Entrepreneur Things venture with just two products to sell – well, actually it's only one product in two colours. It doesn't get much smaller than that. But that's fine. There is an enduring myth that in order to create a successful enterprise you have to risk everything and throw lots of money at it to create something of substance right from the start. In fact nothing could be further from the truth. The biggest businesses can emerge from the tiniest start-ups. It doesn't matter how small you are to begin with; it is what you do afterwards which spells the difference between failure and success.

Starting small is a particularly good idea in the current uncertain economic climate, when no one knows whether their job, or their pension, or even the value of their house is something they can rely on. Small means you can make mistakes and for it not to be the end of the world. Small means you don't have to quit your job. Small means you can do it in your spare time to begin with and only expand when your idea takes off. Small means that starting a business is not a big and scary thing but becomes something manageable and controllable instead.

Kamal Basran's business started out about as small as it is possible to start. A full-time mother of two living in Manchester, she began making samosas after buying some in her local supermarket and deciding they tasted horrible.

Wondering if there would be any demand for a better product, she decided to put it to the test and have a go herself, using the recipes taught her by her mother. As the only girl growing up in a family of four children, Kamal had been expected to help her mother in the kitchen and so learnt to cook using traditional recipes.

She started supplying small batches of her home-made samosas to the delicatessen in her village, Poynton, in Cheshire. Customers loved them. She says: 'I would make samosas on Thursdays to deliver for Friday morning and on Fridays for Saturday morning. Each time they sold out.'

It was the ideal way of starting a venture without any money – because Kamal was doing all the cooking herself and hence donating her time for free, her only upfront costs were the samosa ingredients. She was paid as soon as the samosas were bought by customers. After a few months Kamal decided there was enough demand to start a proper business. Her bank offered to match any funds she put up, so she invested £5,000 of personal savings and received the same again as a loan. The money enabled her to rent a 900 sq ft unit in nearby Stockport, buy basic equipment and employ two part-time staff. Even then, however, she opted to start from a small base. Initially her firm made just three products – samosas, onion bhajis and spring rolls, all vegetarian.

Kamal says: 'We got tiny orders to begin with and some days there was no work to do so we would go home.'

But the big advantage of starting small was that she could learn everything about her products and how the operation worked while the orders were still manageable. This meant that when, in 1987, Holland & Barrett, the high street health food chain, discovered her products in the Poynton delicatessen and asked if she could supply their shops with wholemeal samosas and onion bhajis, she was ready to take on the challenge. Kamal increased her bank loan, moved to a bigger factory and bought bigger equipment, and got to work.

As sales grew, the business took the next step up the ladder – it expanded into chilled ready meals such as beef madras and chicken tikka masala. By 1992 Kamal was making frozen ready meals, too, and rented the factory next door to add more workspace. She also started making a range of other ethnic foods, including Thai, Chinese and Mexican.

Her firm, the Authentic Food Company, which is based in Sharston, south Manchester, now sells nearly a million ready meals a week. It employs 248 people and has a turnover of £42 million a year, and in 2011 Kamal was named Entrepreneur of the Year at the Asian Women of Achievement Awards. All from a single batch of samosas.

Stay flexible

The big advantage of starting small is it means you will be able to change direction easily and relatively painlessly if you need to. If I find my entrepreneur mugs don't sell, it would be very straightforward to start selling something else. I could simply get rid of the mugs I still had either by selling them off very cheaply, or by giving them away. Because I hold hardly any stock, the cost of doing this would be very small, and then it would be straightforward to update my website by replacing the pictures and details of my mugs with another product.

This is the approach Allison Graham took. She decided to start an online business selling children's party accessories after getting really frustrated trying to find enough matching Spiderman-themed paper plates and cups in her local shops for her son Ryan's third birthday.

She says: 'I would go to one shop to find they had the plates but not the napkins, and to another to find they had the cups but not the table covers. But you can't tell a child they can't have Spiderman plates because the shop has only got Peppa Pig, or Bob the Builder. They want Spiderman.'

Allison had no idea if her plan would work, however. So she started the business, Delights, in 2001 with just £500 of stock bought on her credit card – consisting of £50 worth of plates, napkins, cups, tablecloths and party bags in each of ten themed ranges, including Thomas the Tank Engine, Bob the Builder and Barbie. Her husband

Steve and his friend Paul, who both worked for an IT company, came in as co-founders and created the website themselves in the evenings and at weekends, so it cost nothing but their time.

Steve and Paul started doing some free search engine optimisation to raise the site's profile on the internet – meaning the site would appear when people searched for party accessories – and gradually orders began to trickle in.

Whenever Allison took an order she would use the money to buy more stock and gradually began to add other themed ranges.

It was slow going to start with. Allison says: 'I remember wishing we could get one order a day.' But as the venture grew her low-risk approach paid dividends, because it meant any buying mistakes she made did not have lasting consequences. Because she does not manufacture the products herself, Allison can buy just one case of a new theme and try it, so that even if none of it sells the loss is limited to that case. She says: 'If it doesn't work we have only spent a tenner. It is a safe way of doing it.' In fact she has only ever chosen a handful of themes which did not sell well, such as Speed Racer, a children's character.

Allison's cautious start has paid off. Her firm has expanded to include seasonal and wedding ranges, fancy dress, baby ranges and confectionery. It now supplies more than 15,000 products, has an annual turnover of £12 million and employs eighty-five people.

Act big

Starting small doesn't need to mean telling people you are small, however. Providing you act professionally right from the start, no one need ever know.

Sometimes that might mean thinking a bit creatively. When Chris Orrell started a business with his flatmate, Gavin Tett, providing discounted hotel rooms for big companies to offer their staff as a perk, they ran the operation from the flat they shared in Hemel Hempstead in Hertfordshire and only had one telephone line. But they were determined to give the impression of being a large company so they decided to answer the phone under a variety of aliases.

Chris says: 'We had a list of different names and would give them regional accents. For example, we decided the name Paul would be Liverpudlian. If someone asked for accounts I would say I was passing them to the accounts department but it would still be me on the phone.'

He adds: 'We had no set-up at all. It was just mad. To be honest, I am amazed we even got it off the ground.'

His creative thinking worked, however, and their business, Hotelstayuk.com, not only got off the ground, it has thrived and now has a turnover of £3.4 million with clients including John Lewis.

Chris himself is a firm advocate of starting small. He says: 'Whenever I meet people who say they are going to start something and they have put their house on the line, it panics me. Don't go too crazy from the start and do the research. And try to do something you understand and in a market that you have worked in.'

Go one better

The other advantage of starting small is that it is easy to change direction if you find something which works better than your original idea.

When Ian Whybrow started writing books for children about a small boy called Harry, his famous bucketful of dinosaurs was not even part of the story. Ian had responded to a request from a small publisher to produce a Christmassy picture-book story by writing *Harry and the Snow King*, the tale of a small boy who makes do with a disappointing sprinkling of snow by building a snowman on a plate. Not a Stegosaurus or Tyrannosaurus Rex in sight.

It was only when he was shopping in a garden centre in Chelsea, West London that Ian spotted a small boy carrying a seaside bucket. The boy was taking plastic dinosaurs out of it and hiding them under plants to roar at one another. Ian talked to the boy's mother who told him that her son took his bucketful of dinosaurs everywhere with him, spoke to them all the time, sang to them, bathed them every night and knew all their names, even though he was only three years old. It was then that Ian had his brilliant idea.

As he says: 'I thought, there are probably three million books about dinosaurs already but I bet there aren't any stories with buckets in them.' He was able to adapt his original idea of writing about a small boy having a domestic adventure, to writing about a small boy in charge of a bucketful of dinosaurs. That moment of inspiration led to the creation of the incredibly successful *Harry and the Bucketful of Dinosaurs* books and a television series based on them.

The sky's the limit

The most important thing about starting small, of course, is also having the ability to grow very large when the time is right. Starting small doesn't mean staying small, as Allison Graham has discovered. That's not the point at all. It just happens to be a less scary place to begin from before you and your business start scaling mountains.

When I ran a workshop in Frome as part of their Discuss and Do festival I met Sarah Godsill who had started her own business doing drawings at weddings, called Events Illustration. She charges a flat fee to attend the wedding and the reception, where she produces beautiful pencil drawings of the event, typically twelve to fifteen of them, for the bride and groom to keep. After I talked about the importance of having a venture which had the potential to grow, she asked me how she could expand her business. I told her that right now she has plenty of scope to expand: as well as drawing at weddings – which usually only take place on Fridays or Saturdays – she could also offer her services for other memorable events, such as birthdays, or reunions, or even conferences. If she was able to tap into these markets she could potentially find enough work to fill the whole week. And at events such as reunions of old school friends, she could sell copies of the drawings not just to the host, but to everyone present so they could all remember the special day.

The problem of expansion arises, however, when Sarah wants to go beyond this. If she is the only one doing the drawings, then the number of bookings she can take is limited to the events she can physically attend with her sketchpad. With the best will in the world, she can't be in two places at once. Unless she can find a way round this, her business will never be able to expand beyond these limits.

One option would be to train up other people to do the drawings, too – perhaps fine arts graduates from the local college. A good idea in principle but difficult in practice as they will each have their own distinct style – and there is a very real danger they could simply go off and set up in competition with Sarah once they had mastered the skills and found out how the business operates.

A better option might be for Sarah to use her drawing skills to create reproducible items such as invitations, thank you cards and place settings, which she can then sell either via her website or in shops under her own brand name. She will then have something which she can sell over and over again without her actually having to be there. And, what's more, she will be selling into the same wedding market – and often to the same customers.

Tony Stones got his expansion right. At the age of thirty-four, while working for a software firm, he decided to go on a tour of the vineyards in France's Champagne region. He says: 'I did all the touristy bits and I had a few days to spare so I drove round the villages and tasted some of the champagne from the smaller growers. I was amazed by its quality.'

A new convert to the joys of drinking champagne – he was teetotal up to the age of twenty-five – Tony returned home to the UK and tried to buy the champagnes he had discovered, but couldn't find them anywhere. He then contacted the vineyards direct, but they told him they didn't export to Britain because it was too difficult. So he decided to import very small quantities of little-known champagne himself. He started the business, Champagne Warehouse, in 2000 with a neighbour, Alan Swain, and the two of them would take a van over to the vineyards in their spare time and stock up with champagne. They initially sold it via a rudimentary website, in the days before internet commerce was popular. They spent the next three years building up relationships with seven little-known vineyards and eventually got an order to supply a large supermarket chain.

The firm now gets 90 per cent of its sales from supermarket chains. Tony, who took over Alan's share in 2006, now buys from fourteen champagne producers and has also started selling sparkling wines. His business, which is based in Boston Spa, near Leeds, has a turnover of £4 million and employs six people.

It can be immensely exciting to see a venture start to grow from such a small start. However, you do need to make sure you don't make the mistake of growing too fast too soon.

In 2001 Jim Venables and Andy Haywood started a business which found tenants for vacant office space, in the belief there was a need in the market for a broker who spoke plain English. Jim says: 'Rather than talk to businesses about square feet and break clauses and all the jargon, we felt that if we talked to them about their goals and aspirations we could help them find office space.'

They ran the venture from a serviced office in Birmingham Business Park and within a year had signed deals on 700 office buildings, operating on the basis that the office provider only paid for the service once the two of them had found tenants for them.

They were impatient to expand, however, and four years after launching decided to open an office in Dallas, Texas. They soon found they had bitten off more than they could chew.

They initially hired a local person to run the American office for them but when that did not work out, the two of them decided that, instead of appointing someone else local to run it, they would do it themselves, taking it in turns to fly out to Dallas and run the office for several weeks at a time. Amazingly, they did this for more than two years. Jim says: 'I look back now and think, what were we doing? It was just crazy.'

Inevitably the arrangement took its toll on the fledgling business in the UK. Jim says: 'We had two different styles to running a business so for two weeks they would have it Andy's way and he would change things and then I would get back and say, no you have done that wrong. It caused absolute chaos.'

Eventually, in 2009 Andy moved out to Dallas to run the US operation full-time, while Jim stayed in the UK to run the rest of the business from Fazeley in Tamworth. Fortunately both they and their firm survived the experience. Their business Officebroker.com, which finds tenants for offices, now has eighty employees and a turnover of £7 million a year.

ACTION PLAN

▶▶ What are your potential losses if a particular product does not sell? Would the business still be able to survive?

▶▶ Think about how your business could look in ten or even twenty years' time. Does it have the potential to grow big? How big could it get?

▶▶ Being small does not need to mean acting small. Adopt a professional attitude at all times and NEVER apologise for the size of your venture.

CHAPTER 16

THE BUSINESS PARTNER DECISION

Arguably the simplest way of getting all the help, support, skills and practical assistance you need is to get yourself a business partner. Someone to work alongside you and share the day-to-day chores, someone to help you turn your plans into reality, and to come up with lots of good ideas and provide encouragement and enthusiasm along the way.

And the best bit, of course, is you don't even have to pay them upfront for this. You simply give them a chunk of equity in your fledgling venture – which, hopefully, will one day be worth much more than it would have done if you were toiling away on your own.

Well, yes and no. The right business partner will be worth his or her weight in gold. The wrong one will be a disaster and do far more harm than good.

Let's look at the advantages:

▶▶ Business partners can bring skills, contacts and experience

▶▶ You will have someone to bounce ideas off and to share the big and small achievements along the way

▶▶ It will be more fun doing it with a partner than on your own

▶▶ You will get more done as there will be another pair of hands to help with everything from packing boxes and answering the phone to drawing up a business plan and devising a marketing strategy

▶▶ You will not be on your own staring at the wall day after day

But there are potential disadvantages, too

▶▶ You can't just do what you want to do unilaterally – you have to consult someone else on everything and get them to agree first. And if they don't, you will have to compromise

▶▶ They may turn out to have completely different ideas to you about how to run and grow your venture

▶▶ If you fall out it could have disastrous implications both for the business, and for your own confidence. It could be expensive, too.

Certainly it is an issue which tends to sharply polarise people. I asked a small non-statistically significant self-selecting group of entrepreneurs – the people who follow me on Twitter, in other words – what they thought about the idea of taking on a business partner. Some were strongly in favour – 'Much better to have a partner – more ideas, do more work, complementary skills, keep each other buoyant. Can be very wearing alone,' said one. But others were equally strongly against – 'I've got a firm idea of where I want the business to go and don't want to have to clear ideas with a partner,' said another.

Both sides, however, advocated a cautious approach. In other words, if you decide to take on a partner you need to be really, really clear about why you are actually doing it. As one said: 'It's all about adding value. If they can add more than they take out, then yes. Otherwise don't bother.' Another added: 'You have to be very careful and really think it through – as it hurts like hell when it doesn't work out.'

One way to work through the process is to consider the alternatives. If it is purely the conviviality and companionship you are looking for, you might be better off creating an informal advisory board to provide a safe forum for advice and discussion, as addressed in the previous chapter.

If it is simply the idea of having another pair of hands which appeals, you might be better off taking on a graduate intern who can help out where needed – in return for expenses and a small weekly payment – and gain work experience in return.

If you are looking for a set of skills and experience and contacts that you lack, however, then there really is no substitute for getting a business partner. The secret is to make sure that you connect on both a personal and a professional level – and that your roles are clearly defined. There is no point in having two people doing the financial side and no one in charge of design. Or two people keen on production and no one who is good at sales. You will just end up clashing at every turn and not achieving anything.

This is the problem Philip Ross and Martin Izod had to overcome. They became friends while studying product design engineering at Glasgow University. On graduating, they decided to combine their skills to launch a business, Safehinge, making child-friendly door hinges for use in schools and hospitals which prevent children getting their fingers trapped.

As business partners they started out with both of them doing everything, but after a year realised the arrangement was not working and so assigned themselves specific roles.

'For the first year we were treading on each other's toes which felt frustrating' says Philip. 'When we set the roles it was a really good decision because all of a sudden we each had a bit of independence back.'

He is now commercial director while Martin is in charge of the technical side.

He says: 'We have a meeting every Monday to make sure we are moving in the same direction. We are both quite blunt so if there is something on our mind we will say it.'

Now they have sorted out their roles, Philip says the advantages of working together far outweigh the drawbacks: 'The disadvantage is that you are not your own boss and you have to consider the other person. But the advantage is that you get to share your problems and you have two brains thinking about things. The best thing is when you land a key project you get to do the celebratory dance with someone else.'

You also need to think about when to bring in a partner. Ideally it should be earlier, rather than later, in the venture because the longer you leave it the more likely it will have become very much 'your' venture and you might find it hard to give up some control and let someone else – and someone else's vision – in.

Testing it out

I have decided I need a business partner for my fledgling Entrepreneur Things Mug operation. While I love doing some bits of starting a venture – namely talking about it and writing about it – I am less good at doing other bits, namely getting round to adding more products to the website.

Now the mugs are selling well I know the venture has huge potential to expand by selling other entrepreneur-branded products, and I have a good idea of what would work, and what people might want to buy. But jumping from that thought to action requires effort, and, anyway, it would be really nice to share the chores with someone else and to have someone to chat to and discuss everything with. And who ideally might know how to do all the things that I don't.

I mention the idea of finding a business partner to my friend George. He is extremely enthusiastic, both about the potential of the venture, and about the idea of he himself becoming my business partner. To be honest I am quite surprised he would be interested because he has lots of other much bigger projects going on, but it would be really fun having him as a partner. We start discussing how it might work in practice. We agree to think about it more over the weekend and have another chat on Monday after George has had a look at the Entrepreneur Things website.

George rings on Monday morning as arranged. The first thing he is says is: 'I am bowled over by its simplicity.' I say thank you. At least I think it was a compliment.

There is one big advantage of taking on George as a partner and one big disadvantage. The one big advantage is that George knows lots of people who have started up businesses of their own so if we need help with any aspect, whether search engine optimisation, or website design, or administration, or whatever, George will know just who to ask.

The big disadvantage of taking on George as a partner is there is a very real danger we won't actually get round to doing anything at all, and will sit a round drinking and chatting every time we meet instead of getting down to work.

He asks me how many mugs I have sold. I tell him, and then I give him the passwords to access my Google Adwords page and my Google Analytics page so he can see for himself how many people have been accessing the website and which page they stop at and so on.

We discuss how a partnership would actually work in practice; basically this boils down to how we can work most efficiently together. We decide we should initially spend every Monday working together in the same office, then communicate by phone and email for the rest of the week. That way we can discuss everything face to face once a week and set out a plan for the following few days.

We also agree that the primary aim of the business is to grow it to a point, say within five years, where we can sell it on to someone who can take it to the next level. It is important to ensure that we have a common goal.

He says he will go away and think about it and get back to me. And I say that's great, hoping he will say yes.

When choosing a business partner it is important you don't choose one just because you think they will be fun to have around and share your adventure with; you also need to choose someone you think will be best for your business.

Unlike hiring someone for a job, the problem is that usually you do not have the luxury of choosing between several potential contenders – you are merely trying to decide whether the person standing in front of you will do a better or worse job than someone who isn't them.

The one essential is that it has to be someone you totally trust. I know that George and I feel the same way about lots of issues and having seen the way he deals with things I trust him 100 per cent.

One way round the trust issue is to go into partnership

with a member of your family. The other big advantage of having your brother or sister, for example, as a partner is that any success the business achieves will be shared and enjoyed equally, and so is less likely to lead to resentment and family rifts if it takes off and does well.

Chris Edwards's father was so worried about the potential problems which could arise if only one of his sons created a successful business that he stepped in to prevent such a scenario from arising. Along with his wife, he used to run a market stall in Wakefield, selling household items. As children, Chris and his younger brother Laurie would often help out on the stall and grew up with it being very much a central part of their lives. So when Chris, who had taken over the running of the market stall, decided to start a business by opening a shop selling household goods, and employed Laurie to help him, his father immediately spoke up.

Chris says: 'My father said, "I can't have one son working for another, but if you tell me how much it has cost you, I will give you half and you can become partners"'.

He did and together Chris and Laurie gradually opened more shops, in 1997 turning them into pound shops, where everything cost £1. Laurie has been a partner in the business, Poundworld, ever since. The firm now has 104 shops and a turnover of £135 million a year.

Where things go wrong

Unfortunately partnerships do go sour, sometimes disastrously so. Whenever you read about a business arrangement in the newspaper in which the two sides 'decide to go their separate ways', or choose to 'pursue their own interests', you can be pretty sure there has been some massive bust up or major disagreement which has led to that point. After all, if a venture is proving to be successful, why would anyone voluntarily choose to walk away, unless the prospect of working with the other person had become completely unbearable?

Assuming both sides are still talking to each other, it is possible to come to an arrangement whereby one side buys the other out and continues on alone. When James Nash started his bike rack business, Bike Dock Solutions, he persuaded two friends from college, Josh Coleman and Craig Jones, to join him. They each invested £10,000, a combination of savings and borrowing from their parents.

A year into the venture, however, cracks began to appear in the partnership when it became clear they had different ideas about how the venture should be run. So Craig left and the other two bought him out for £20,000, borrowing the money from their parents. It was a painful experience for everyone, though.

James says: 'It was a difficult time because he wasn't just a business partner; he was a good friend.'

Nevertheless, James and Josh divided the work between them and have since gone on to start up two more ventures, which collectively with the bike dock business have a turnover of £3.4 million.

Two months after agreeing in principle with George that he should come in as business partner, I start to get cold feet. Not least because I haven't heard from him once in the intervening time since we first agreed in principle about the idea, which I feel rather suggests a lack of enthusiasm on his part.

I also realise I am in serious danger of ignoring the advice I give to others. When thinking about the pros and cons of getting a partner, what you really need to do is think back to when you were at secondary school and the teacher asked you to find a partner to work on a geography project with. Think hard – did you love the idea of working together with someone, or did you secretly loathe it? Personally, I hated it, every time. Geography projects, physics experiments, history presentations, whatever it was, I always wanted to do it on my own. Whenever I had to do it in pairs with a partner I immediately lost interest. Just couldn't be bothered. My reasoning was that I wanted to be judged by my own efforts for something, whether that turned out to be good or bad. I couldn't think of anything worse than having either to share the glory or share the blame if it all went wrong. I preferred to have all or nothing. And I always hated having to compromise about what we were going to do in the project because, inevitably, the other person would have different ideas.

It's a good test by the way: try it. You will know instantly whether you are better off in a partnership or better off doing it on your own.

So what on earth was I doing taking on a business partner in real life, on a project where the stakes were far higher than for a geography project on volcanoes? I needed more time to really think this through. So I sat down and wrote an email to George, explaining that I had decided to postpone any decision about taking on a business partner for the next few months. I hoped he wouldn't mind too much.

I received his reply a few hours later. 'I am actually very, very stuck into one big project at the moment so relief is right. Good luck with everything.' Phew! So that's all right then. I'm on my own once more. Back to work.

ACTION PLAN

▶▶ Write a list of why you would like a business partner and what qualities they would need to make it work.

▶▶ Think back over your life – do you generally achieve things better alone or with a partner?

▶▶ If you have someone in mind, invite them to join your informal advisory board first (see chapter 14). That way you can get to find out how they operate – and how they would run your venture – before having to commit.

CHAPTER 17

HOW TO SPEND NOTHING EXPANDING YOUR BUSINESS

I have received an intriguing email from the owner of a small firm which prints calendars. Nigel wants to know if I would be interested in selling entrepreneur calendars along-side my entrepreneur mugs. The calendars would feature a useful piece of advice from a successful entrepreneur to illustrate each month.

He writes: 'Looks like you need a few more products so how about The Entrepreneurs Calendar? I'm sure we could get one together pretty quickly. No need to buy any upfront as we can print them on demand and mail them direct to clients, they can even be personalised to individual clients. What do you think? Let me know.'

My first thought is: brilliant, it sounds perfect. It would be my second product and one which would be ideal for budding entrepreneurs working from home and staring out of the window in search of inspiration. Now they can stare at my calendar on the wall instead and get real inspiration from the uplifting thoughts on it. And if I don't have to buy any calendars in advance that is doubly perfect, because there will be no upfront cost and the whole thing won't need any money to get off the ground. I could simply email Nigel with details of orders as they came in and he could print the required number of calendars and send them out to the customer himself. How cool would that be? It would be the ultimate no-risk no-cost solution for both sides.

As for selling them, I could simply take some photos of the calendar and upload them on to my Entrepreneur Things website. I already have lots of inspiring quotes from successful entrepreneurs which would be perfect to put on a calendar, and lots more people I could call to get more if I run out. Suddenly I can't wait to get started.

My second thought is: it's already November, there is no way we can get this off the ground in time to be able to sell calendars for the coming year, 2012. We would really have to have them ready to buy within a couple of weeks if we have any chance of selling any. I can't think of anything less useful than a calendar which goes on sale sometime mid-February.

But when I speak to Nigel he is willing to give it a try, to get a calendar ready before December and the pre-Christmas chaos. And he has other exciting suggestions, too; suggesting a range of entrepreneur stationery with diaries, notebooks, notepads and greetings cards. He says it may be possible to design these in such a way so that they, too, can be produced on an 'on-demand' basis, thereby reducing the initial outlay to zero. He also points out that doing it this way means all the products will be able to be personalised.

It's time to get to work. I send Nigel twelve quotes for him to design a calendar around and wait to hear back. (My favourite is a quote from Bruce Bratley, who founded the First Mile recycling service: 'Keep making decisions. You might make some bad decisions but you have got to keep making them. So many people just stop making decisions and they wonder why their business is failing.')

Inevitably, though, it doesn't happen in time. Nigel disappears into the ether, laden down with other projects. I don't chase him, December comes and goes and my calendar remains an idea which has yet to happen.

By January I am still as keen as ever on the idea and get in touch with Nigel again. I'm thinking that we could definitely do a calendar for 2013, and even before that we could do a calendar which runs from September to September for budding entrepreneurs who are studying at college or university at the same time as starting a business. There are a growing number of students hoping to create a money-making venture which will not only fund their studies, but which might even do away with the need to find a job on graduation, too. Nigel sends over some designs, and we start talking.

I have had another idea, too – canvas shopping bags with the word entrepreneur printed on them, perhaps in the same cut-out version as the design on the mugs, so the words are cut out of a block of colour. Once again, being able to order in small quantities will be essential. I start asking people if they can recommend a supplier who could do this.

The secret to expanding your business, of course, is not just to find products or services which you can add on for little or no cost; it is to find products which customers will actually want to buy. I was asked to speak at an Entrepreneur Live event organised by Tutor2u for sixth formers studying business studies and economics for A level. The event was held on three consecutive days in London, Birmingham and Manchester and each time I talked to the students about my mug venture and asked them what other products I should add. They shouted out lots of suggestions, from computer mouse mats to hats, bags, pens, T-shirts, mats, desk tidies and stress balls. The follow-up question, however, was harder: which of these products do you think people would actually be prepared to pay money for?

Initially, I myself thought mouse mats would be a good idea, so I asked the firm that makes my mugs to send me some samples of mouse mats so I could decide which one I preferred. But after testing out the idea on a few friends, I discovered that people are forever being giving free mouse mats for promotional purposes these days, so no one would ever need to buy one themselves. And, more intriguingly, apparently no one actually uses a mouse mat these days anyway – except me. So that idea was quickly shelved.

Be creative

You may also be able to find a new market for your products simply by repackaging the things you already sell in a way which will appeal to a new group of customers. Stephen Williams has brought a bit of magic to his wine merchant business, The Antique Wine Company, with an idea which cost him no money to implement at all. A former life assurance salesman, Stephen decided he wanted to sell wine for a living after realising it would be much more enjoyable selling something that people actually wanted to buy, as opposed to insurance, which people begrudged spending money on. He initially sold a range of high-quality wines, and then, as the supermarkets began to sell good-quality wines, too, and made the market more competitive, Stephen started specialising in rarer, older vintages.

But when the internet made it much easier for customers to seek out rare wines for themselves instead of relying on a wine merchant to do it for them, Stephen realised he needed to stay one step ahead. So he began to create vertical collections of rare wines, notably the prestigious and sought-after Château d'Yquem, with bottles of the same wine produced in consecutive years. He sold one such collection, which included a bottle of Château d'Yquem from every year from 1855 to 2005, to the glamorous Grand Hotel du Cap Ferrat on the Côte d'Azur for close to £1 million, far more than the individual bottles themselves would be collectively sold for.

The joy of this is that it is the input of 'free' elements such as patience and time, contacts and know-how which adds the value. As Stephen says: 'I find that a lot more enjoyable than just trying to undercut my competitors by £50 on a case of five-year-old wine.'

Exporting for beginners

At first glance, exporting sounds like an unlikely thing to be able to do without any money. Not so, provided you go about it the right way. When James Watt wanted to start exporting the beer he made at his Scottish brewery, Brewdog, he lacked two key things – any knowledge of international markets and a marketing budget. Undaunted, Watt simply chose the two regions of the world with the biggest and most vibrant beer culture – Scandinavia and America. Then he found out the names of the people who wrote the most respected online blogs about beer in both countries, contacted them and offered to send them samples of his beer.

The tactic worked. The bloggers tried his beer and loved it, and then they wrote complimentary pieces about them in their blogs, which were read by all their followers. That meant James could then go to an import distributor in Sweden, for example, and show them the blogs and tell them they really should stock his beers because 1,000 people a day were now reading these influential blogs raving about his beer. The importers took the hint and started importing Brewdog beer – and so for the cost of sending a case of beer to Sweden, James was able to start selling to key export markets, in a really short space of time.

Brewdog beers are now sold in nineteen countries, and the business, which is based in Fraserburgh, is the largest independent brewery in Scotland, selling more than 500,000 bottles a month. It has an annual turnover of £3.7 million and employs thirty-seven people. As James says: 'Don't accept that things have to be done in a certain way. Why not do things differently?'

I've deliberately made my Entrepreneur Things website look export friendly so it will attract overseas customers. I've arranged it so that customers buying my mugs can choose to buy them in pounds, dollars or euros, and the right value postage will automatically be added on by PayPal at the paying stage so I can send my mugs to customers anywhere in Europe and America as well as the UK. I can add on more countries later. The most important thing is that by including these currency options on my website I am sending out a clear message to potential customers that I am a global business and am happy to send my products anywhere in the world, if that's where people want them. Clever.

But not quite clever enough, as it turns out. Because then I get an email via the site from someone called Marc which is entitled, 'Can you help?' It reads: 'I am in the UK and would like to buy one of your wonderful mugs and have it delivered in the US. Do I have to pay in dollars to ensure the US delivery charge is attached or is this for US customers only?' Good question. Will I have to change the whole website so people can choose to pay in one currency and yet have it delivered in another country? How will that even work? How will my payment system be able to cope with such a multitude of potential options? How do other businesses cope with this?

Then I think, let's deal with one customer at a time. Maybe I can just get Marc to pay in pounds and also pay the delivery charge in pounds, and I can send him an additional payment request via PayPal for the difference in cost between the UK postage of £2.48 and the US postage of $8.60 – around £3, I calculate. Not very elegant but simpler than changing the entire payment structure of the website.

That £3 represents virtually all the profit I would make on selling the mug. But then I think, well, it's nearly Christmas. So I reply: 'I think the best thing to do is to pay for it in pounds with the UK postage fee attached, and put the US address on the order – seeing as it's the festive season I would be very happy to cover the difference in postage and send it to the US for you at no extra charge.'

So Marc orders his mug. And then he emails me to say that he is sending it to his brother in Washington – who just happens to be the President of Global Entrepreneurship Week. Wow. And how brilliant. I am so glad I didn't quibble over that £3.

It also makes me realise that the best way of dealing with unusual queries is to do it on an individual basis rather than attempting to implement a 'one size fits all' policy. So I simply amend the product ordering page on my website to read: 'Please contact us if you have any delivery queries'.

The best thing about making an online venture global is you don't even really have to think about whether and when – or even where – you are going to start exporting. You simply make it possible for people to order your products from overseas by including the right delivery options and charges, and then wait to see where your orders are coming from. If you start noticing a lot of orders from a certain region, then you can tweak your website to appeal even more to that group of people. If your website provides information on festivals around the world for example, then a surge of interest from people living in Spain could be rewarded with more information about festivals in Spanish-speaking countries.

Crunch the data

Thanks to Google Analytics you can even see where the people who are looking at your site live, even if they don't actually buy anything. I just looked at Google Analytics for entrepreneurthings.com – it tells me that so far I have had a total of 979 visitors to my website of whom 859 came from the UK, 25 from the US, 9 from Australia, 8 from India and 6 each from Brazil, India and Russia. I'm not quite sure what use all this is at this stage, but if I suddenly got a spike in visitors from Russia then it might be worth me thinking about providing a Russian translation on the pages, or bringing out a mug which says entrepreneur in Russian.

You can break down the figures for the UK further, too – in my case I see that, of the 859 visitors from the UK, 821 were from England, 26 were from Scotland, 11 from Wales and 1 from Northern Ireland. Again, if the numbers from Scotland were huge, say, I could think about introducing a Scottish flavour to the website, to help Scottish visitors respond to it favourably. And you can even break down the figure for England into regions – I see that Entrepreneur Things is big in London, not surprisingly – but that the website also has some fans in Southampton and Manchester.

When Christopher Ward started selling his watches via mail order in newspapers he realised a lot of orders were coming from America. When one of his US customers rang him up, he discovered his watches had attracted the attention of an online watch forum based in America called Timezone. Some of the people leaving comments on the forum had taken apart his watches to check on the quality of the internal movements and liked what they found so much they wanted to start a Christopher Ward thread where people could comment on the watches. Christopher agreed, and the thread now has 3,500 members.

For Christopher, the interest from America has not only been good for sales; the feedback provided by the forum has also proved invaluable. He says: 'They tell us when we get something wrong and when we get it right. It is an early warning system.'

If you want to be a bit more proactive about exporting your products and services than simply waiting for customers to find you, the best place to start is UK Trade & Investment, a government-backed service with international trade teams based in forty offices around Britain, including dedicated sector specialists. It provides a range of schemes, many of them free, specifically designed to help British companies looking to export. The Passport to Export scheme, for example, offers free capability assessments, mentoring and support in visiting potential export markets. The Tradeshow Access Programme offers grants of up to £1,800 to enable small firms to attend overseas trade fairs.

The calendar trail seems to have gone quiet again for the moment, so I decide to pursue plan B – selling canvas bags with my entrepreneur design printed on one side. A friend directs me to a website which turns out to sell every kind of canvas bag you could wish for – carrier bags with short handles, shoulder bags with long handles, both with and without extra depth. Even better, there is no minimum order so, as the website points out, I can buy from one to millions. This is fantastic news. I choose a strong heavy-weight canvas shopper bag with long handles made from natural cotton and email the company for a quote.

At which point I fall slap bang into the hurdle that all small firms trying to get off the ground fall into – the price versus quantity vortex. Although I can indeed theoretically order any number of bags from one to millions, it turns out that if I order ten bags printed with my design on one side, for example, it will cost me £75.61 including VAT, working out at a cost price of £7.56 per bag. But if I order 100 bags, say, then the cost falls to £313, working out at a cost price per bag of just £3.13. That's a big difference.

What's more, when I speak to Paul, the web sales manager at the company, he tells me that bags ordered in small quantities are printed using heat transfer, whereas bags ordered in large quantities are printed using a process called screen printing, a superior method which produces a more vibrant colour. The reason for this is there is an upfront cost of creating the screen, which doesn't make financial sense for small volumes but does when spread over larger volumes. He also says that the minimum order for the screen printing method is 100, and that is only for one colour, so even if I order 100 I will still have to choose between getting them done in the deep pink or the blue I used for my mugs. I can't have some of both unless I order 200 bags.

Obviously on a cost per unit level it makes sense to order 100 rather than ten. But that's £313 tied up in bags, a significant sum of money at this stage, and what if they don't sell? I particularly wanted to be able to buy a small quantity to be able to test them out first, so that if they didn't sell it wouldn't much matter because I wouldn't have lost a lot of money.

All of this also affects the price I can charge, too. I wanted to sell the canvas bags for £8, because I think that is the most anyone will realistically be prepared to pay for a canvas bag, even if it is the hard-wearing kind and even if it does have the word ENTREPRENEUR on the side. But if I only order ten, they will cost me £7.56 each to buy before packaging and postage, so if I price them at £8 I will actually be selling each one at a loss.

I realise I have several choices:

▶▶ buy ten of the bags with the inferior printing for very little outlay to test out the market and sell them at a loss (not a good route to take, ever, and not really a fair test anyway if the bags don't look as nice as the screen printed ones);

▶▶ price the bags at £10 rather than £8 and hope I will still find people willing to buy them at that price; alternatively, buy thinner canvas bags which will be cheaper but poorer quality and less hard-wearing;

▶▶ buy 100 bags printed using the superior screen-printing method, hope I make the right decision between deep pink and blue, sell them for £8 each – and hope that people buy them.

Hmm. Happily, when I ring up the mug printing firm to find out the exact colour shades they used for the mugs, they tell me that they have started printing canvas bags, too. They use screen printing and they can use the same designs that they created for my mugs. Their minimum order is still 100, but at least I can have half of them in deep pink and half in blue. And, even better, I don't have to think about this any more. Total cost £381.60, equal to £3.81 per bag. I say yes and hope that people like entrepreneur bags as much as they like entrepreneur mugs.

ACTION PLAN

▶▶ Think about how you will be able to expand your business – by offering more products or services? Or by selling into new markets, or new locations?

▶▶ Find out where visitors to your website are coming from. Does your website cater for their needs or do you need to tweak it?

▶▶ Research the cost of sending your products to customers overseas – it may be that a courier service can offer a cheaper price than Royal Mail, for example, although make sure it is both secure and reliable.

CHAPTER 18

HOW TO GET POST START-UP FUNDING

However difficult it is to get funding to start up your business, the good news is that once you are up and running, it becomes a whole lot easier. This is because people feel much more comfortable investing in something they can see already exists and actually works, and because it is a lot easier to explain to people what your business does when it is actually doing it. Telling people you are going to make a fortune selling fluorescent socks is a lot easier when you can actually show them that you are already selling 100 pairs a day and that many of your customers are regulars.

The even better news is that, although high street banks are generally reluctant to lend to small firms these days, several new alternative funding options have emerged to help new businesses to grow.

The equity option

One such alternative is crowd funding, which uses the power of the internet to pool together lots of very small amounts from individuals to make a sizeable sum which can then be invested in small firms to help them grow. In return for their investment the individual gets a tiny stake in a business which they hope will grow to be worth a lot more by the time the business is eventually sold.

Even though it is still very new, crowd funding is proving to be an interesting way for entrepreneurs and small firms to raise cash with relatively low risk on both sides.

When Alex Kammerling needed £180,000 to grow his small business, Kamm & Sons, which makes and sells an alcoholic drink he invented called Kamm & Sons Ginseng Spirit, he didn't even bother asking his bank manager for a loan. Instead in 2011 he sought finance through Crowdcube (Crowdcube.com), a UK-based crowd funding service which brings together enterprises looking for funding and individuals who like the idea of being part of an entrepreneurial venture.

Ventures looking for funding pitch their idea on the website, ask for funding of at least £5,000, and set a deadline. Individuals can then invest anything from £10 upwards in return for shares in a venture. There is no maximum limit that can be raised by a business, although under Crowdcube rules businesses seeking money have to secure investor backing for the full amount they seek by the deadline in order to get the money. If they only managed to get pledges for some of that amount, they won't get any of it. The reasoning behind this is that investors are investing their money on the assumption that the entrepreneur will be able to use the total investment specified to grow their venture – if they don't actually get much of the money, that makes the prospects for the business a very different proposition. Crowdcube makes its money by taking 5 per cent of any successful fundraising as a fee.

Alex succeeded in getting the full £180,000 he asked for and so the eighty-five investors who put up the money via Crowdcube now collectively own 23 per cent of his venture.

Alex says it is a model which really appeals to him: 'I would much rather give equity away than take out a bank loan. I have opened myself up – my business plans are on the website and all my projections of what I am doing. That kind of honesty is a very modern way to do business. It means you have to be completely transparent. I was very nervous about it but it has been brilliant.'

Sue Acton also managed successfully to secure funding through Crowdcube for her Fairtrade body care business, Bubbles and Balm. In 2010 she became Crowdcube's first success story when she raised £75,000 by giving away a 15 per cent stake in her firm. In total eighty-two individuals invested between £10 and £7,500.

Because investors are taking equity rather than lending you money, if your business fails, you do not have to repay the money.

Since it was set up in 2010 Crowdcube has managed to raise £2.5 million for fourteen small firms.

Some entrepreneurs are coming up with crowd funding schemes of their own to raise money for their ventures. One of them is Naked Wines, an online wine retailer. While traditional wine merchants buy wines they like and sell them on to customers, Naked Wines uses the collective buying power of its customers to commission wine from independent producers.

It means the wineries can focus on making the product rather than selling it, while customers benefit from lower prices because there are no marketing costs to cover.

Naked Wines, which is based in Norwich, now has 50,000 'angel' customers – investors, in effect – who each pay £20 a month into an online account, which they can use to spend on wine from Naked Wines. This fund, equal to about £1 million a month, is used to support independent winemakers by paying them during the production process.

Rowan Gormley, one of the co-founders of Naked Wines, which was launched in 2008, says the unique business model has only been made possible by the crowd funding – also known more generally as crowd sourcing – possibilities created by the internet. 'This business could not have existed ten years ago. There is no way we could have done this without the internet. The advantages of crowd sourcing are that a thousand people can achieve together what one person cannot on his own.'

So far the model is working well. Naked Wines has more than 100,000 customers, including the 'angels', and supports thirty-eight suppliers who make wine for the company. In 2010, its second year of trading, it turned over £10 million.

The borrowing option

Another new funding option is Funding Circle (Fundingcircle. com). It also uses the principle of getting lots of people to put up small amounts to amass a sizeable sum, but in this case individuals lend money rather than take equity. Borrowers must be established businesses with at least two years of filed accounts and can ask for between £5,000 and £250,000 for a period of one, three or five years. Individual investors can choose to invest a minimum of £20. The rate of interest is set by the lender, whose offer is accepted or rejected by the firm seeking finance.

So far some 569 small firms have received combined funding of £23 million through the site since it was launched in 2010, and to date all requests for funding have been met in full. Small companies borrowing this way through Funding Circle have so far included a boatyard on the Thames, an ironmongery firm, online retailers and coffee shops.

Unlike an equity arrangement, if your business fails you will still need to repay the money you have borrowed to the extent that it is recoverable, perhaps by selling the business assets.

Do it yourself

Some small businesses are also creating their own funding ideas, often based round the idea of raising money from their customers.

Will King, whose business King of Shaves makes shaving

oil and razors, successfully raised £627,000 from around 400 customers in 2009 by way of a 'shaving bond'. Customers could invest between £1,000 and £5,000 in a non-transferable, non-convertible three-year bond which paid them 6 per cent interest a year and shaving products worth £30–£60 a year. The secret to successfully raising cash this way, says Will, is to have already established a strong following among customers who trust you and your products – and a strong underlying business which will be able to repay the bond at the end. He says: 'It's a great way to bypass the banks and go straight to your customer base to raise money.'

Caxton FX, a foreign exchange provider, also chose a bond model to raise money from private investors.

The firm, which was started in 2002 by Rupert Lee-Browne, managed to raise £3.9 million by issuing a bond. The money will be used to provide working capital to expand the business, which has a turnover of £400 million. Investors put in between £2,000 and £50,000 in the four-year bond in exchange for a gross annual return of 7.25 per cent.

Rupert says: 'The bond really fit our ethos of giving customers much better value than the banks currently offer. It was a logical extension of what we do. We wanted to create a more entrepreneurial approach to fundraising which would cut out the middlemen and provide investors with a rate of return which would beat the UK high street banks.'

A good place to look for alternative funding options is Fundingstore (Fundingstore.com), a website which aims to help small firms find funding by bringing together all available options in one place.

There are, of course, some risks attached to raising funds in a non-traditional way – unlike banks, alternative finance providers such as Funding Circle and Crowdcube are not at present regulated by the UK government. Instead they are self-regulated through an umbrella organisation set up by themselves called the Next Generation Finance Consortium. This is more of a concern to the lenders than the borrowers, i.e. the small businesses, as it means lenders are not currently covered by the Financial Services Regulation Scheme, but it is worth bearing in mind.

Friends and family

Of course, the first place most entrepreneurs look for funding is from friends and family. Again, though, as this is also an area not bound by external regulation, you do need to set ground rules which all sides are happy with, because if you don't do it right it could end up creating more problems than it solves. Borrowing from friends and family can be a minefield, leading to arguments, breakdowns in relationships and even legal action. What happens if, say, a relative or friend who has lent money believes he then has a right to get involved in decisions about the direction of the venture? Or if they suddenly decide they need the money back? Most importantly, what happens if the business fails? So you need to tread very carefully – and you need to write everything down.

The secret is to make it very clear what transaction is taking place – is it a loan which needs repaying? If so, over what time period? And will you pay interest? And what happens if you can't repay the loan?

Or is it equity? In which case you need to make it absolutely clear that if the venture fails the money will be lost for ever.

When it is done right, it can work well. When Jamie and Helen Read's bank turned down their request for a £3,000 loan to start a dance and drama school, they asked their family for help instead. Parents, grandparents, aunts and uncles agreed to give £15,000 between them as an open-ended, interest-free loan.

That funded the opening of their Read Dance & Theatre College in Reading, which runs a one-year foundation course for 200 students who want careers in musical theatre, as well as dance classes for children.

'Our problem was that banks didn't seem to understand what we were trying to set up,' says Jamie. 'We looked at all sorts of options, such as business angels, but in the end we went cap in hand to our family. We planned to make a formal presentation but everybody just went, oh, shut up and come round for a cup of tea. We were very careful to ensure that nobody was lending under duress or giving more than they could truly afford.'

The arrangement has proved a success. The Reads regularly update relatives on the school's progress and have already repaid most of the loan.

Unsurprisingly, the biggest problems arise if the business turns out not to be the success it was hoped to be. Ensure that friends and family could afford to lose what they have lent you. Don't ask them to re-mortgage their homes or put all their savings into your venture because if it goes wrong the fallout will be horrendous. Not only will you lose your business, you may lose family and friends, too.

And be honest about the risks. It is far better that people go in with their eyes open. Often family and friends are willing to support a new venture, thinking it is going to be the next Facebook, without fully appreciating the risk involved.

Emotions can run high and relationships be tested even when a venture succeeds. A relative may have been repaid with interest, but they still feel aggrieved that they are not able to share in its future progress.

One way round this is if the business shows signs of taking off and being a success, then instead of paying back all the loan, offer family lenders a slice of equity in return for the amount outstanding. It may ultimately cost you more but if it keeps the peace then it's a small price to pay.

The best way to prevent problems is to make the financial arrangement with family and friends as formal as possible. Try to take the personal element out of the relationship. Put everything in writing, offer to pay them interest and approach it as you would an external funding relationship.

That is what Amanda McCaig did. When the former teacher decided to start selling merino wool clothing from New Zealand, she funded the venture with £6,000 borrowed from her husband, Andrew.

Even though they had been married for more than thirty years, she approached the loan as a formal business transaction, setting up a standing order from her business bank account to make repayments each month until the loan, plus interest, was repaid.

'It was set up properly from the start. You have to do that and then it never becomes personal. You don't want to fall out over money – it's a stupid thing to do,' says Amanda.

It took her a year to repay the loan, and then she borrowed a further £20,000 from her husband, a geologist, to fund expansion. Again, she set up a monthly standing order and has now virtually repaid this loan.

On the back of the initial loan, she has built up her Leeds-based enterprise, Chocolate Fish Merino, to sales of £80,000 a year, with exports across the world.

For Amanda, the advantages of borrowing from a relative were clear: 'I knew I was dealing with somebody trustworthy and ethical, whereas a bank could suddenly decide to call in its loan.'

One more way of bringing funds into your business once it is already up and running is to use invoice factoring. At its simplest, invoice factoring means that when you send an invoice to a customer requesting payment, you are able to get a percentage of the amount you are owed immediately, long before the bill is actually paid, which could be several weeks later. You have to pay a fee for the service but for some businesses it can make a big difference to cash flow.

Most banks provide an invoice discounting facility or you can opt for an online version such as MarketInvoice (Marketinvoice.com), which allows small business with unpaid invoices from larger firms to auction these online to institutional investors.

ACTION PLAN

▶▶ Decide what you actually need the money for – and for how long. If it is only for a short period, a loan would be better than giving up equity.

▶▶ Think about whether your customers could provide the funding you need – through upfront investment in a collective fund or bond, say.

▶▶ If you are borrowing from friends and family, put everything in writing so both sides know what is involved. Be clear whether it is a loan or equity.

CHAPTER 19

BUT WHAT ABOUT THE RECESSION?

At first glance starting up a business in the midst of a harsh economic climate might seem like a crazy thing to do. But there can actually be considerable advantages to starting a venture in a recession.

Indeed, a quick glance at some of the world's most successful companies shows that many of them started up in tough economic times. Burger King, FedEx and Microsoft all did, as did MTV, Disney and General Motors.

There are several reasons why recession can be good for start-ups:

▶▶　　Because if your venture can survive in the bad times when every order is an order hard won, just think how it will fly in the good times when customers seek you out rather than the other way round. Plus by then you will have much more experience to be able to make the most of it. Many of the companies who started up in the mid-1990s boom years, particularly the first wave of dot com companies, discovered that when the good times ended they were totally ill equipped to handle the situation when the downturn hit because they had no concept of having to go out and fight for sales instead of expecting them to just happen.

▶▶ Because your costs are likely to be much cheaper – the price of raw materials, office space, and so on are all much more likely to be open to negotiation in tough times than in good because there will be fewer customers for them – and so suppliers will all be competing for your custom. You are also more likely to be able to attract high-quality people to work for you, who in good times may have been employed in jobs elsewhere. Added to this are the huge number of qualified graduates coming out of colleges and universities who would normally have walked straight into a well-paid job without so much as a backward glance. This amazing talent pool is at your disposal. It's a real opportunity.

▶▶ Because with everyone adopting a pared-down mentality there is no need for you to spend money on flashy offices or fancy company cars. In these hard times customers not only do not expect ostentation, they do not want it. And they particularly don't want to feel that their hard-earned cash is going on unnecessary glitz. It just feels all wrong. Which, of course, is fantastic news for you and your minimalist pared-down start-up.

Susie Fletcher launched her first business, Amelie and Rose, an online lingerie company, bang in the middle of the tough times in 2011. She used to work for Nottingham City Council but decided to give it up to study corsetry at college before starting her own venture. She designs all the garments herself, which are made with silk and lace, and gets them made by a local factory.

She is unfazed about the prospect of starting out in the middle of the worst recession in living memory.

She says: 'I don't think I am going to be selling my lingerie like hot cakes in the first week and I am going to have to be quite canny about how I develop the business. But I am optimistic because I think if you have got a product which people like, then there will still be interest in it. And if you look globally there are countries where economies are growing and there is huge potential.'

Susie, who runs the venture from her home in Derby, has been careful to spend her small start-up budget only on essentials. She says: 'I think that if you can develop a business in a recession then it will stand you in good stead in the future because you are going to come out with some great skills. I am quite realistic that things are going to be difficult for a while, but what are we supposed to do instead – just sit at home?'

Another first-time entrepreneur undaunted about taking the plunge is Tony Curtis. He has just launched his first enterprise, Alago, to sell the heated gloves he spent five years inventing. A former educational behaviour specialist who worked with children in schools, Tony came up with the idea for his gloves while watching his son's hands turn blue while playing rugby. He patented the process he invented and now has three products ready to sell – rugby gloves, football gloves and gardening gloves. The heating pads within the gloves are activated either by putting them in a microwave or by pressing a button on the glove; the heat lasts for an hour.

He, too, is acutely conscious of the need to keep costs down and already has distributors lined up in America, Ireland, Austria, Belgium and France.

Like Susie, he, too, is hoping international sales will offset the impact of recession in the UK. 'If I was just going to sell direct in the UK then I would be beholden to that market only. But I can sell to Europe and Canada and Japan too so I am covered for a certain amount of sales,' he says. 'I am still getting interest from retailers and wholesalers so although it is not going to be a huge start, it is going to start comfortably. And from that I can build a much stronger brand for when we finally start coming out of the recession. I am fairly confident.'

Tony, who is running the venture from the family home in Bristol, says: 'It certainly gives you an impetus to find sales wherever you can. We have been using a lot of social networking to get our name out there. We are on Facebook and Twitter and Linkedin and Google Plus.'

For some, the recession is merely seen as an inconvenience – far more important is the timing in their own life.

Claire Hall launched her business, Percy's Vodka Iced Tea, in 2011 after working on the idea in her spare time for several years. She makes the drinks – currently in two flavours – lemon and lime, and mango with orange – in a local factory near her home in Boston, Lincolnshire. She sells them online via her website and at food and drink shows around the country. She is in the process of taking on a distributor and is keen to start exporting.

Claire, who started up with a combination of savings, grants and borrowing, says: 'I don't even think about the recession. I really think that if you have got a good product, and if there is a market for that product, then it will sell. People still have money. Yes, they are a bit more careful what they spend it on, they don't want to spend it on rubbish, but they will spend it. People are always going to want to try new things.'

She adds: 'I think it is a great time to start a business. Being small and having a niche product is definitely an advantage. People don't particularly want a mass-produced product now, they want to know where it has come from.'

Seize new opportunities

As well as being a great opportunity to shrink start-up costs, recession can also produce new opportunities. When times are tough people want good value, no-nonsense products which will last. They want products which will save them money. And they sometimes want low-cost products which will cheer them up – hence the traditional rise in cinema tickets and lipsticks during a recession. They don't want to pay for frills and unnecessary things but a little bit of inexpensive fun amid all the grey is always welcome, too. So if you can find a product or service which fulfils that brief then you are in a good place already.

Recessions also tend to shake out a lot of poorly run firms – bad and sad for those companies, but a wonderful opportunity for new entrants to the market who can see a way of doing things better, or differently. As old-style businesses go bust, new niches and opportunities emerge – a large firm laden down with high fixed costs might go to the wall, but that opens up opportunities for new entrants with lower overheads and more flexibility. And that is no bad thing. It opens the door to innovation, to new ideas, and to better ways of doing things.

Outsider Tart, an American-style bakery and caterer which started five years ago, is currently growing 40 per cent year on year despite, or perhaps because of, the recession, and now has a turnover of £650,000. The business, in Chiswick, west London, was one of the first to introduce whoopie pies, a popular American treat, to Britain. Having seen the success of the cupcake here, Outsider Tart promoted the whoopie pie as the cupcake's natural successor and they are now one of its bestsellers.

David Muniz, who founded Outsider Tart with David Lesniak, says: 'Innovating and doing different things has helped us stay ahead. It is a combination of good planning, good product and a lot of luck.'

One unexpected success has been their cookery classes.

When a television channel in America broadcast a piece about Outsider Tart, people called from all over the world to book places, and within two weeks all classes for the next year were fully booked.

David says: 'We started teaching because we figured that when money gets tight it becomes more of an indulgence to go out for a meal and people want to start making stuff for themselves at home instead. We hadn't planned on doing it but it has turned out to be quite good for us.'

Yes, starting up in a recession can be a nerve-wracking ride. And doing it in a buoyant economy instead would perhaps make for a less terrifying start. But most of us don't have the luxury of being able to wait for the good times to roll again. You can't simply put your life on hold in the hope that external factors beyond your control will improve. Because they might not get better any time soon, and by then you will be that much older, and that much more fearful of doing something bold. One good thing about starting in a recession is, because there are fewer jobs around, you are actually theoretically giving up a lot less than you might have done. If that highly paid high-flying job isn't an option any more, the decision not to take it becomes an awful lot easier.

The bottom line is, don't let the capriciousness of the world economy dictate how you run your life. If it's the right time for you personally to start a business, then that is far more important than anything going on in the outside world.

Worst case scenario

I am a great believer in imagining the worst-case scenario in any situation and then working out how to deal with it. This approach drives some people mad, particularly a lady I met recently at a conference who wasted no time in telling me that negativity was self-fulfilling and that I should only ever think positive thoughts and focus on positive outcomes as these will attract more positive energy towards me – or something like that anyway.

But I don't regard thinking about the worst-case scenario as being a negative thing to do; I see it as being sensible and useful because it means that you are facing up to your worst fears, looking them straight in the eye and tackling them head-on instead of hiding away from them. It is positive, practical and empowering, and I recommend it to you.

Let's apply my approach to starting a business in a recession – what is the worst that can happen? Well, the worst is obviously that it will fail and take all your savings and time with it. So okay, let's think about that. What would that mean? Would it really be so bad? Obviously you would be worse off in a strictly financial sense, but hopefully not by much if you have taken my advice and started small and not invested your life savings in your project. What's more, you would also have learnt an enormous amount about how businesses do and don't work, and you would have shown yourself to be resourceful and capable of thinking in such a way to get a venture off the ground.

Even more importantly, you would have proved to yourself – and others – that you have the guts to take a leap into the unknown, and see where it takes you. No mean feat, and all of these are skills and attributes which are likely to appeal to a potential employer. So at the very worst you will really stand out from the job-hunting crowd if you decide that running your own business is not for you and you would prefer to work for someone else. Your CV will come alive with your description of how you went about starting a business and what skills and knowledge you learnt along the way, and that passion and enthusiasm will shine out to an employer. And you will have gained valuable skills and experience if you do decide to have another go at starting a business.

Best of all, you will have found out if being an entrepreneur really is for you, instead of constantly having that niggling little voice in your ear saying, I wonder what would happen if . . .

See, the worst case scenario doesn't look quite so scary now, does it?

Actually doing something, rather than constantly putting it off and putting your fingers in your ears and saying 'lala-lalala' whenever people ask what happened to your dreams, can be immensely satisfying and life-affirming. Even if you fail, and even if the dream turned out not to be quite as you imagined. Because at least you tried. And that puts you head and shoulders above every else who didn't.

Remember, if you can cope with the worst-case scenario then you really have no excuse not to try. The economic climate is just a backdrop. You can succeed with, or without it, in spite of it, or because of it. Now let's get to work.

ACTION PLAN

▶▶ Think about whether people are more or less likely to buy your product or service when times are tough. Why?

▶▶ Consider whether you will be able to export your product or service – is there likely to be a demand for it overseas?

▶▶ Write down: what is the worst thing that could happen if you start a business? How would you cope with that?

CHAPTER 20

ONWARDS
AND UPWARDS

So what of my fledging Entrepreneur Things business? Well, it's still pretty teeny tiny but I'm delighted to report that it is doing really well. I feel immensely proud of it. It now sells mugs and bags and there are lots more products to be added, too, just as soon as I get round to sourcing them, or else finding an enthusiastic business partner who will do it for me. I've also got lots of ideas about how to promote and sell my products.

The other thing I have discovered, and you will, too, is that starting a business without any money is not just good for the bank balance – it can actually be good for the enterprise itself, too, because a lack of cash often forces you to be more creative. Good ideas invariably emerge from trying to find new ways of doing things. It's the difference between buying a round-the-world plane ticket and staying in smart hotels along the way – or working your way round the world while staying in hostels and sleeping on people's sofas, so that the whole venture ends up costing you nothing. Yes, the second option will involve a lot more effort and forward planning, but it will also ultimately result in a far more enriching and eye-opening experience.

So you see, you have two choices. If you don't have any money then you can either forget all about the idea of starting your own business, sit down on the sofa, get sad and cross and pack your dreams back into a box. And resign yourselves to working for someone else for the rest of your life.

Or you can simply roll up your metaphorical sleeves and get on with doing it anyway. As you will have discovered from this book, right now there is an enormous amount of free advice, resources and technology out there to help you on your way. It would be silly to let it go to waste. All you need is to create the right framework, have the flexibility and willingness to think creatively – and the determination to make it happen.

There is one final thing to say. In the rush to find ways of not spending money, it is important to keep things in perspective. The winner is ultimately not the one who manages to spend no money at all; the winner is the one who creates a successful business. There is no point in spending endless hours trying to work out how to trademark your logo design, file your business tax return or incorporate a video into your website, in order to save every last penny, if these are things you do not know how to do or do not feel comfortable doing. You will end up with poorly protected intellectual property, unreliable accounts, an amateurish website – and feeling completely traumatised at the pain you have had to put yourself through.

Even worse, you will also have wasted valuable time in which you could have done a huge amount of things which you were good at towards getting your business off the ground – and possibly made more money than you would have saved anyway.

So save money where you can, structure your business in a low-cost way and always look for the free or cheaper alternative, but never skimp on the legal stuff, and above all, never lose sight of the bigger picture.

Finally, don't stop believing. Don't stop believing in your ability to make something special happen, and above all don't be embarrassed about getting excited about lots of ideas and projects which don't end up working out, or which you don't end up pursuing. And whatever you do, don't feel you have to pursue them simply because you have been going on about them for such a long time. Remember, the only thing worse than having lots of ideas which don't work out is having no ideas at all. Accept that your friends will mock, and that your family will roll their eyes every time you tell them you have had a new idea for a business – and get over it. Do not be put off, and whatever you do, do not give up having ideas and checking them out to see if they will work.

When Darren Richards was trying to come up with an idea which would make his fortune he was always looking out for the next big idea. He tried everything from a loyalty card for high street shops to Japanese electronic toys in his search for the opportunity that would make his fortune. He says: 'I tried so many different things that my friends would say, oh here comes Darren, I wonder what new idea he has today.' But he ignored their taunts and kept on coming up with new ideas, until he finally found one that worked. And Darren is the one laughing now – he sold the online matchmaking business he created, Dating Direct, for £30 million.

Good luck, and do let me know how you get on – feel free to email me at contact@rachelbridge.com. Or, of course, via entrepreneurthings.com . . .

APPENDIX

USEFUL RESOURCES

99designs.co.uk

Accessstorage.com

Adwords.google.co.uk

Argos.co.uk

Asda.com

Big Yellow Self Storage – bigyellow.co.uk

Companies House – companieshouse.co.uk

Conceptcupboard.com

Crowdcube.com

Discuss and Do Festival – discussanddo.co.uk

Ecademy.com

Efaze.com

265

Enterprisenation.com

Equifax Find Out – findoutinfo.com

Facebook.com

Federation of Small Businesses – fsb.org.uk

Floodlight.co.uk

Foodfrombritain.co.uk

Forum of Private Business – fpb.org

Freecycle.org

Fundingcircle.com

Fundingstore.com

Godaddy.com

Google Plus – plus.google.com

Google.com/analytics

Google.com/webmaster

Heart of England Fine Foods – heff.co.uk

HMRC – hmrc.gov.uk

Inspiringinterns.com

Intellectual Property Office – ipo.gov.uk

Johnlewispartnership.co.uk

Linkedin.com

Lowcostnames.co.uk

Marketinvoice.com

Moonfruit.com

Mywarehouse.me

Odesk.com

Paypal.co.uk

Peopleperhour.com

Peter Jones Enterprise Academy – Pjea.org.uk

Princes Trust – Princes-trust.org.uk

Safestore.co.uk

Sainsbury – Supplysomethingnew.co.uk

Sedo.co.uk

Shell-livewire.org

Startupbritain.org

Tesco.com/regionalsourcing

Tutor2u.net

Twitter.com

UKTI.gov.uk

Waitrose.com/sourcing

Wayra.org

Wix.com

Wordpress.org

Youtube.com

ENTREPRENEURIAL BUSINESSES MENTIONED IN THIS BOOK

AddMaster – addmaster.co.uk

Alago – alago.ltd.uk

Amazon – amazon.co.uk

Amelie and Rose – amelieandrose.co.uk

Ample Bosom – amplebosom.com

Antal International – antal.com

The Antique Wine Company – antique-wine.com

The Authentic Food Company – theauthenticfoodcompany.com

The Backland Studio – thebacklandstudio.com

Bed of Nails – bedofnails.org

Bike Dock Solutions – bikedocksolutions.com

Binifresh – binifresh.com

Bio City – biocity.co.uk

Bog In a Bag – boginabag.com

Bompas and Parr – jellymongers.co.uk

Brewdog – brewdog.com

Bubble and Balm – bubbleandbalm.co.uk

Buxton Pickles – nortontownsend.com

Caxton FX – caxtonfx.com

Champagne Warehouse – champagnewarehouse.com

Chocolate Fish Merino – chocolatefishmerino.co.uk

Christopher Ward – christopherward.co.uk

Corn Again – cornagain.co.uk

Crimson and Co – crimsonandco.com

Delights – delights.co.uk

Duvet and Pillow Warehouse – duvetandpillowwarehouse.
co.uk

Enhance Image Consultancy – enhanceimage.co.uk

Enternships.com

Entrepreneur Things – entrepreneurthings.com

Events Illustration – eventsillustration.co.uk

Everbuild Building Products – everbuild.co.uk

Frank & Faith – frankandfaith.com

Frequency Telecom – frequencytelecom.co.uk

Gingerlily – gingerlily.co.uk

Go Native – gonative.com

Gower Cottage Brownies – gowercottagebrownies.com

GTech – gtech.com

Hallam Internet – hallaminternet.com

Hardnutz – hardnutz.com

Hotelstay UK – Hotelstayuk.com

Hotel TerraVina – hotelterravina.co.uk

Hunter Jameson – hunterjameson.com

Kamm & Sons Ginseng Spirit – kammandsons.com

King and Allen – kingandallen.co.uk

King of Shaves – shave.com

Lisa Shell Architects – lisashellarchitects.co.uk

Mindcandy – mindcandy.com

Naked Wines – nakedwines.com

Nancy Leigh Knit – nancyleighknit.co.uk

Need A Cake – need-a-cake.co.uk

Notonthehighstreet – notonthehighstreet.com

Officebroker – Officebroker.com

Outsider Tart – outsidertart.com

Part Eaz – parteaz.co.uk

Percy's Vodka Iced Tea – percys-t.com

Poundworld – poundworld.net

Read Dance and Theatre College – rdtc.org.uk

Redemption Brewing – redemptionbrewing.co.uk

Results International – resultsinternational.com

Rodial – rodial.co.uk

Safehinge – safehinge.com

St Helens Farm – sthelensfarm.co.uk

Salty Dog – saltydog-grrr.com

Sapphire Education and Training – sapphireeducation.com

Says Shoes – saysshoes.co.uk

Scott Dunn Travel – scottdunn.com

The Silver Apples – thesilverapples.co.uk

Snow PR – snowpr.com

Spabreaks – spabreaks.com

The Stag Company – thestagcompany.com

Think – think.eu

Time Capsules – timecapsules.co.uk

Triumphant Events – triumphantevents.co.uk

We Are Social – wearesocial.net

WEGO Couriers – wegocouriers.co.uk

We Make London – wemakelondon.co.uk

INDEX